If You're Trying To Teach Kids How To Write . . .

Revised Edition

... you've gotta have this book!

By Marjorie Frank

Incentive Publications, Inc.
Nashville, Tennessee

ACKNOWLEDGEMENTS and PERMISSIONS

The author and publisher wish to thank the following publishers, authors, and agents for permission to reprint selections in this book:

THE CONDE NAST PUBLICATIONS, INC. for "The Soldier," by Rencie Farwell from "Teacher's Priceless World: Where It Is Always Spring," by Kay Boyle, *Glamour Magazine,* March, 1963. Courtesy GLAMOUR. Copyright ©1963 by The Conde Nast Publications, Inc.

HOUGHTON MIFFLIN COMPANY for excerpts from *Smashed Potatoes.* Copyright ©1974 by Jane Martel. Reprinted by permission of Houghton Mifflin Company. All rights reserved.

HARPER-COLLINS. Excerpts from *Cross Your Fingers, Spit In Your Hat: Superstitions and Other Beliefs,* collected by Alvin Schwartz. Copyright ©1974 by Alvin Schwartz.

DANIEL LUSK for "Children There Are Words," from *Homemade Poems* by Daniel Lusk. Copyright ©1974 by Lame Johnny Press, Associates. Reprinted by permission of Daniel Lusk.

OREGON DEPARTMENT OF EDUCATION for "The Oregon Direct Writing Assessment Analytic Scoring Guide." Reprinted by permission of the Oregon Department of Education.

Special thanks to all the young writers who have made such delightful contributions to this book.

Illustrated by Kathleen Bullock and Judy Howard
Cover Design by Marta Drayton

Library of Congress Catalog Card Number: 95-75474
ISBN 0-86530-317-7

PRINTED IN THE UNITED STATES OF AMERICA

CONTENTS

Do any of these sound familiar to you?

"But teaching writing is such hard work!"

"I don't have the time! There are too many other things to teach!"

"My kids say they can't think of anything to write."

"What's important—the ideas and creativity or the skills?"

"My kids groan when it's time for writing. To tell you the truth, so do I."

"It's pulling teeth to get kids to revise."

"But my kids are too young to write!"

"I have this kid who just WON'T!"

"My students are too shy or fearful to express themselves."

"It takes them so long to write."

"I always run out of ideas by October!"

"Help! I have to give grades for writing!"

"I can never get them to write on their own."

"What do we do with the writing when it's finished?"

"If I focus on teaching skills, won't I stifle creativity?"

"UGH! Assessment! It takes so much time to score all those papers!"

"Now I'm expected to do portfolios! Seems like more work!"

*They surely are familiar to me! Some of them are my own excuses for avoiding writing instruction. Others are rationalizations for failures. **ALL** are the questions and fears and concerns collected by eavesdropping on teacher-friends over the past several years.*

Oh—how much has happened in the world of writing since 1978 when I wrote the introduction to the first edition of this book.

Since then, the topic of how to teach writing has burst open—and what a wonderful and exciting explosion it has been. The process approach to writing, the writer's workshop settings, writing across the curriculum, portfolios and writing assessment are common in the vocabulary of classroom teachers today. Dozens of states have flourishing writing projects that train more and more teachers each year. The successful use of writing portfolios is rapidly spreading. New models for analyzing and scoring writing abound. Many programs for authentic writing assessment are giving writers feedback that truly improve the processes and skills. Gifted educators such as Donald Graves, Lucy Calkins, Peter Elbow, Nancie Atwell, and Thomas Newkirk have spent thousands of hours writing with young people and have gone on to put their experiences into writing-- giving immeasurable help and support to teachers all over the world.

We've come a long way as teachers of writers, haven't we? My discussions with teachers all over the country tell me we have. My own experiences, particularly with college students who have now benefitted from years of writing process instruction, tell me something good has happened. There certainly is an awareness of the importance of writing and of good techniques for teaching it.

And yet, when I talk with teachers about writing, I still hear a lot of questions and pleas for help. Some of the questions are the same ones that I wrote on the opening page to the first edition of this book. But now there are more.

Last fall, about three weeks into a course I was presenting to classroom teachers on Writing Portfolios, one teacher came to me sheepishly after class and asked, "You keep talking about the writing process, but I don't really know exactly what the writing process is." Oh-oh! I learned my lesson. Since then, I start every course or workshop with a good lesson on the writing process.

Many teachers are just learning about the process approach while others are more sophisticated in their experience of teaching writing. We're at many different places in our various journeys of writing with kids.

However, as I talk to teachers all over the country, I hear more likenesses than differences. In general, I hear that you

... are still concerned about exciting writing experiences and the fresh ideas that get kids writing and loving it.

... are just as concerned about the technical skills of writing.

... want to know how to combine the freedom of expression with the discipline of completing and perfecting a written piece.

... want to help kids grow at handling all parts of the writing process.

... are trying out some new things in writing: performance assessment techniques, portfolios, and more integration of writing throughout all disciplines in the curriculum.

... are working to expand your students' experiences with writing in many genres and for many purposes.

... always need support and encouragement for the job of mixing young people with writing.

So here I am, again, writing about teaching kids to write!

My interaction with teachers struggling to do a good job of writing with kids had a lot to do with bringing me to write this book 15 years ago. And more of that interaction has inspired me to re-think, expand, and revise this book today.

There are two other forces behind my words in the pages ahead:

ONE is the **JOY** that fooling around with words has added to my life, combined with the personal growth that's been stimulated by many experiences with language. I was lucky to have a mother who shared with her children her love of language. She played word games, baked riddles and puns into cookies, taught us poems and Bible verses on family trips, made up tongue twisters, wrote idioms on the kitchen chalkboard, gave dramatic readings of ridiculous rhymes and tales at community functions, and freely shared with us her own writings.

The **OTHER** is the **ENJOYMENT** that I've gained from writing with kids in my own classrooms, kindergarten through college. Some of the most rewarding moments I've had with students have revolved around experiences of self-expression. Those were the times that brought about the unfolding of persons. Those were the moments that led to the most startling improvements in skills and self-confidence. And those were the times that left some of the nicest memories!

*Let me confess at the beginning that I've been on a sort of personal **promote-writing-in-the-classrooms-of-the-world** campaign for years. My soap box message is that kids CAN learn to express themselves effectively and comfortably in writing—even in the midst of a fast moving culture that fills their lives with electronic games, cellular phones, and portable CD players.*

I know it can happen. I've seen it happening again and again ... kids writing and growing and publishing. We CAN have a generation of persons whose thinking skills, writing skills, and life skills are well-developed, if we are gutsy enough to take on the challenge of creating serious writing experiences in our classrooms.

Now, I am NOT going to tell you any nice syrupy tales about how quick and easy it is to write with kids. I'm NOT going to try to entice you with any instant cures for your fears or writing problems in your classroom ... because...

... I believe that writing takes discipline.
... I believe that teaching writers takes work!
... I believe that a teacher of writers needs also to be a writer.

I AM going to enthusiastically share with you my strong biases that...

... teaching writers, and being a writer, is also fun and fulfilling.
... it's a kind of work less dreary than most of us think.
... it is worth the energy it takes.
... YOU can enjoy it and grow as much as the kids!

Since my goal for kids is *to build a generation of word-lovers...*

... persons who are sensitive to themselves and their worlds and to the powers of their language,
... persons who are willing and able to put into words their strongest beliefs, biases, ideas, feelings, wonderings, and wildest fantasies,
... persons who are experienced in thinking about their own expression and able to make constructive evaluations and improvements in their own work,
... persons who can enjoy learning and growing and writing in the company of others who are doing the same, responding to and encouraging each other ...

... my goals for this book are ...

... to get YOU excited about writing—just for yourself!

... to turn you on to the joys of writing with kids.

... to encourage you to take the risks and plunge into the work of teaching writers and enjoy the results of that risk: freer flow of expression, greater growth in language skills, closer human contact, and just plain fun!

... to give you tips for handling the whole writing process in the classroom.

... to offer you enough ideas and possibilities for motivating writing that you will never run out of inspiration!

... to help you expand your use of good writing assessment and writing portfolios to help your students grow as writers.

... and, possibly, hopefully, to give you a whole new look at writing—maybe even to entirely revolutionize your thinking about what it is!

So what about you? What brings YOU to this book? *Are you...*

... looking for someone to convince you to plunge in?

... needing a way to combine ideas with the technical skills of writing?

... hoping for a whole bunch of stimulating new ideas?

... searching for a new way of thinking about writing in your classroom?

... after help for your writers in trouble?

... due for a freshening of your attitudes or a reminder of your own talents as a writer or teacher of writers?

... needing some help in managing the whole writing process with your kids?

... looking for help with assessment or portfolios?

I think you can find some help with all of these needs and others. Just make use of the Table of Contents to seek the chapters or sections for YOU. This is a "treatise" on writing with kids, so you may want to read it all the way through. It is also a handbook, with each chapter ready when you need it to help out with a specific part of the job of working with writers.

May you have many rich writing sessions as I have had with kids, and many, many more...

Marjorie Frank

"I feel like I'm typing myself into this story."

"Finally, someone listens to ME!"

"Writing is telling stuff you know is important."

"My pencil lets out ideas I would never tell anyone."

"It's like taking the lid off yourself."

"When you write—it's only YOU on paper."

"When I wrote this poem, I felt like I was looking in a mirror."

"Writing puts me out there. It's a little exciting. It's a little scary."

"Real writing is not always about nice stuff."

"Writing lets other people in on your dreams."

"Writing tells secrets."

14

1
The
ROOTS

"Can I really teach somcone else to write?"

Where Writing Starts
What Do You Believe About Writing?
So You're Trying To Teach Kids How To Write ...
What Does It Mean To Teach Writers?
In The Writing Classroom
The Climate Where Kids Will Dare To Write
Take Another Look At Writing
Over 200 Alternatives To ... *"Write A Story"*

Fog

You never know about fog. It sneaks in
and out while you are sleeping. It plays
hide and seek around the buildings. It
reaches its fingers through the streets,
and wraps the whole world outside with
a grey blanket.

        dictated by...Sara Joy, Grade 1

How To Tell......

There is a strange quiet in your house.
Your father is reading the newspaper but not turning any pages.
Your mother is fixing dinner and slamming every cupboard door.
Nobody notices that you didn't hang up your coat.
Nobody reminds you to practice the piano.
That's how to tell an argument between your parents.

        Sherrie, Grade 7

Once, I didn't mean to—but that was that!
I stepped in a bathtub and sat on a rat.
I'd rather take a shower with a lion or a goat
I'd rather take a swim in a shark-infested moat
Than slide beneath the bubbles to shampoo my head,
And latch onto the tail of a rodent that's dead.
It felt a little squishy,
It didn't squirm a bit.
I bathed last night with a deceased rat—
And that—was—it!

        Tom, Grade 7

Question

  Grown-ups always rush around
  Will they never learn
  To slow down?

        Angela, Grade 4

My Lunch

Thick, soft, spongy sourdough
Leafy, crunchy lettuce greens
Ripe RED tomatoes
Oozing, goozing, gooey mayonnaise
Spicy salami
Chewy, stick-in-your-teeth cheddar cheese
Creamy, tangy mustard
Sturdy, thick sourdough bottom

        James, Grade 9

The Most Important Thing

The main thing about celery is not the green
Or the munch
Or the crisp
Or the crunch
The main thing about celery is the thing that
stays with you long after the celery is gone.
The main thing about celery
is the strings.

        a group of 2nd graders

WHERE WRITING STARTS

How does this kind of writing happen?

What is it that...

... unleashes these opinions ... insights ... questions ... clever ideas

... and helps kids find the words to express them?

I can tell you that...

... it's NOT the district or state curriculum guide.

... it's NOT your school's writing goals.

... it's NOT the writing section of your language text.

... it's NOT the school style book.

... it's NOT the list of 4th grade or 11th grade writing skills.

... it's NOT the district (or classroom) portfolio system.

... it's NOT your scoring guide for writing assessment.

It is NOT any plan, program, checklist, handbook, or set of goals. What causes (or allows) this kind of writing to happen is...

... two groups of warm, living, breathing human beings...

... KIDS and TEACHERS.

These are the real ROOTS of writing.

You're just beginning a whole book full of my ideas about how to help kids grow in writing. You'll see that I am **very concerned** about kids learning the writing process and perfecting writing skills... and about teachers setting goals, teaching specific skills, making use of portfolios, and designing a sound assessment system.

But writing is about human expression. It takes human beings to do it. And it takes live persons to help kids learn it. And so, the systems are NOT the heart of your writing program. The humans are.

WHAT DO YOU BELIEVE ABOUT WRITING?

Almost 20 years ago, I began leading seminars and workshops for teachers on how to write with kids. Doing this forced me to put down in speeches and on paper what I, Marge Frank, believe about writing. Again, when I wrote this book in 1978, again in 1994 when I began this revision, and many other times in between (especially when I've started writing with a new group of kids or teachers), I've revisited and re-examined those beliefs. Each time has taught me plenty about myself both as a writer and a teacher of writers.

It's impossible to create a book about writing without expounding on many of my own beliefs. You've already figured that out, I'm sure. To share some of them boldly, I've boxed and labeled them, *"BIAS,"* which is just what they are—strongly-held, personal beliefs about writers, the writing process, or the teaching of writers.
Here's the first one...

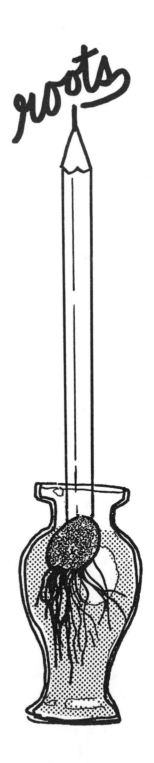

> ### BIAS #1
> ### YOUR JOB ISN'T TO TEACH WRITING
> *If you enter the classroom expecting to focus on teaching writing skills and processes to the kids, you've got the job description all wrong.*

"Wait a minute!" I can hear you saying. *"This is a book called, If You're Trying To teach Kids How To Write... and now you, Marge Frank, are telling me I've got it all wrong if I think I should teach writing to kids? Are you crazy?"*

Here's what I want to tell you: STOP thinking about yourself as *teaching writing*. Notice the title of this book. It begins, *"If you're trying to teach KIDS..."* This is my bias: **You don't teach writing. You teach WRITERS.** And, believe me, there IS a world of difference between the two.

What are **your** biases? We each come to the teaching of writing (or any subject) with a well-rooted lifetime of experiences, attitudes, feelings, beliefs, and talents in that area. It isn't often that we stop to take inventory of those—or consider how they affect our success or our influence on the young writers who are our students.

If you're going to work with writers, please get to know your own *writing* attitudes and beliefs, fears and abilities. Please think about what it means to you to *teach writing*. Here's why...

- Your view of writing WILL seep out, no matter how hard you may try to contain it, and influence your students' views.

- Your view of yourself as a writer will contribute to your bravery (or lack thereof) in trying new writing experiences with students.

- The confidence you have (or don't have) in handling the writing process will affect the way your students learn it.

- Your ideas about what writing is, what it is for, and how writers grow will shape the whole experience students have with writing in your classroom: when and where and how often they write; what they write; the kinds of input and response they receive; how the writing is shared; how and when and how often and by whom it is evaluated; etc.

- The importance you place on writing will determine the amount of dignity and value your students accord it.

- Your expectations for your students' writing will affect their own expectations and their performances.

- And ... the strengths and talents you already possess will be the forces that set directions for your students' growth.

RIGHT NOW ... STOP ... and take an inventory of yourself as a writer and a teacher of writers. Turn to the next two pages and carefully consider each question. Try to answer them honestly, thinking about what each one means for your comfort with the writing process and your connection with young writers.

19

SO YOU'RE TRYING TO TEACH KIDS HOW TO WRITE...

First, what about you ... as a writer?

Do you like writing?

Do you think writing is hard, or easy, or both?

How do you feel about yourself as a writer?

Do you write beyond what's needed for your teaching tasks?

Have you grown as a writer in the past 5 years? How?

Can you identify your strengths and weaknesses as a writer?

And what about you ... as a teacher of writers?

Do you like teaching kids about writing?

Do you think of your students as writers?

Do you believe kids CAN learn to write (and revise)?

How much importance do you attach to writing in the classroom?

How much writing instruction do you provide your students?

What do you believe "a writing experience or lesson" involves?

What is your greatest strength as a teacher of writers?

What goals do you have for writing in your classroom this year?

Do you consistently find and use fresh ideas for writing?

Are you able to allow expression of all ideas and emotions?

How often do you write WITH your students (and enjoy it)?

Do you listen—really listen—to your students?

Do you believe your students' ideas are as valid as your own?

Do you compare one student's writing to another's?

Do you accept that every student will NOT be excited by every writing experience you plan?

Are you comfortable when students choose to go another direction than the one you've provided for writing?

20

And what do you think about your students as writers?

Do you know what your students feel about writing?

Do your students see themselves as writers?

Do they write for themselves? for you? for someone else?

Is writing pleasant? … dreadful? … boring? … exciting? for them?

What kinds of past experiences have your students had with writing?

Do they feel comfortable expressing themselves in your classroom?

Lurking in every classroom are the seeds and roots—the basic beginnings and life support—of writing. Many people think that the "root stuff" of writing is stuff like the language arts curriculum or the English course outline, your collection of wonderful writing ideas, your past training, and the yearly goals for writing.

You've read my BIAS # 1, so you know I firmly believe that's not at all where the roots lie. Roots, after all, are living. Writing has its deepest beginnings of life in the human beings that live inside your classroom walls. What happens in your classroom with writing **has everything to do with you and the kids.** When instruction focuses on the skills … the goals … the plans … the systems—it often becomes mechanical, detached from kids, lifeless. When it focuses on the **persons**—the writers, it's just the opposite—it has **life!**

The tiny sample of kids' writing on page 16 springs out of the fertile garden of the imaginings and opinions of kids nourished and tended by caring teachers and peers who've joined together to write.

Understanding these roots won't produce instant growth in writing. But I can guarantee that NOT understanding or IGNORING these roots—the **persons** in the classroom—WILL hinder your writers, their growth, and your teaching.

WHAT DOES IT MEAN TO TEACH WRITERS?

Think about growing a garden. You may have a great plot of healthy, well-prepared soil and a top-rate, up-to-date gardening manual. You may add to that: sturdy tools, lots of time and hard work, faithful fertilizing and weeding. But if you don't have any seeds—anything with life potential—it's going to be a pretty boring garden.

Skills and techniques and processes are merely TOOLS for use by writers. Only when you think about teaching humans do the tools have value and purpose. They help grow something living. No matter what great supplies, techniques, and setting you have—if your **writers** aren't at the center of the plan, it doesn't do much good to have all those other great tools or soil or hard work, does it?

I doubt that any person can actually TEACH another to write. As teachers, we can only...

… unleash the forces of expression.

… awaken sensitivities to the world, to selves, and others.

… prod awarenesses of feelings, ideas, sensations.

… offer forms for combining words and putting ideas together.

… expose and demonstrate a process for gathering, organizing, and expressing those ideas.

… show them how to use tools for saying things clearly.

… consistently expose them to good, effective, interesting writing.

By suggesting that you think about teaching WRITERS instead of WRITING, I do not mean to diminish the skills and techniques and processes of writing. I'm just asking that you think a little differently about all that *stuff* you know is good to teach. Realize that those rich ideas and experiences, tools or techniques of writing, and lessons on the writing process … are all just **supplies** you make available for use by growing writers.

Now, as you read this book, I'm sure you'll catch me talking about "teaching writing" instead of "teaching writers." It's such a natural phrase for this topic. Whenever I refer to "teaching writing" or state, "teaching writing skills," I will be thinking of this in the sense of teaching kids to handle these skills for THEIR uses as writers. Never are the skills sacred, or even useful, in isolation from their use by real live persons expressing real ideas.

something that matters...
...communication...
...satisfying...nurture
...OPINIONS...
...QUESTIONS...JOYS...
...self-significance...RELEVANT
...real-life stuff

BIAS #2
LIFE IS THE "STUFF" OF POETRY
Writing involves kids with the REAL happenings of their minds and worlds and hearts. They MUST be able to connect their writing to their real lives, real concerns, real feelings.

One of the best lessons I've learned about teaching writers was taught to me by a usually teacher-pleasing nine-year old. For at least a dozen writing lessons, Kim sat with a blank paper (and an even blanker expression) and repeatedly insisted, *"I can't think of anything yet."* One day my gentle prodding turned to an impatient: *"Well, when ARE you going to write something?"* Her almost inaudible answer came, *"When you ask us to write about something that matters."*

Ooooo, that one hurt. She was right. I had concentrated ONLY on the happy and light and beautiful. In so doing, I had insulted my students by acting as if strong feelings—hurts and fears and questions and frustrations and joys—real-life stuff—didn't exist for nine-year olds.

Now I know better. I know that when kids perceive that their opinions, real thoughts, wildest ideas, and deepest concerns are not going to be accepted, then a whole part of themselves—that force which creates poems and protests, questions and fantasies—will at best linger underground and at worst wither. But I know, too, that when writers find approval for telling what's in their heads and hearts and dreams, and are given the tools to tell it precisely and fluently...

... communication that is satisfying to human needs flourishes.

... the writing process becomes relevant.

... respect for the technical skills of expression grows.

... self-awareness, self-acceptance, self-significance bloom.

And that's what this book is about ... giving kids the nurture, the freedom, and the tools to let their voices be heard.

IN THE WRITING CLASSROOM

So writing is a way for living, breathing, thinking people to express any number of the thousands of possible ideas that brew inside minds and hearts. Then what does this mean for a teacher sharing a classroom with a bunch of kids?

> ### BIAS #3
> ### KIDS NEED TO BE FED A MIXTURE
> ### OF GREAT IDEAS & GOOD TECHNIQUES
> *The writing classroom must be a stimulating, comfortable place that combines sprightly ideas with serious instruction in technical skills.*

This means that if you step into a classroom where instruction and practice centers around real, live **writers** (teacher included), you'll find a lively combination of...

... lots and lots of samples of literature shared and read

... lots of talking and sharing of ideas and beliefs

... planned instruction in the writing process

... much practice in using the writing process

... kids or groups practicing individual writing skills

... teacher-initiated group writing experiences

... kids working on various parts of the writing process

... the whole group writing collaboratively

... kids writing independently ... often ... in journals and other ways

... kids writing in pairs or small groups

... plenty of reflecting on writing ... by the whole class or groups

... kids working on portfolios (selecting, organizing, reflecting)

.. kids conferencing about writing with teacher or peers

... kids revising writing ... with partners or small groups

... teacher-led mini-lessons on specific writing skills

BUT ... kids don't automatically know how to do all this—use the process, collaborate, reflect, conference, revise, tackle specific writing skills, prepare and organize or evaluate portfolios, etc.

Which leads me to another of the biases about writing that I hold to quite stubbornly...

BIAS #4
THE TEACHER MAKES A DIFFERENCE
Young writers learn best in the company of an adult who willingly guides and eagerly joins them in the processes of writing.

No matter how fantastic the writing program or how exhaustive the list of writing topics or how detailed the list of writing skills, it comes down to this in the writing classroom...

... there are just plain some things that can be done best by a real, live human being, such as a teacher.

Your writers need you hanging around. Because it's YOU who can...

... spill your love of language into their lives and dazzle them with the wonders and powers of words.

... surprise them (repeatedly) with all different kinds of writing.

... romance them into forming or remembering their own good ideas and having the courage to put them into words.

... BE THERE during the **whole** writing process ... walking through it with them again and again.

... ask the questions that help them to reflect and edit and evaluate and polish their writing ... and to respond to others' writing.

... dignify their writing by seeing to it that they get a chance to share it and show it off.

.. MODEL for your students what it means to be a writer.

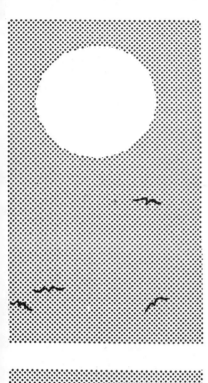

> ### BIAS #5
> ### WRITERS NEED SAFETY
> *Fluent, effective communication flourishes in an environment where persons can risk exposing their REAL lives ... where the act of telling what they are really thinking is treated with utmost respect.*

In such an environment there is...

- **Acceptance ...** of selves, individuals, ideas, differences.
  The climate says to kids: *"You are valued."*

- **Open Communication ...** support, caring, and plenty of straight talk about things that matter.
  The climate says: *"You are important enough to listen to ... and I trust you enough to tell you some treasured thoughts, too."*

- **Freedom ...** to try, to risk, to question, to explore, to think unconventional thoughts, to fantasize, to be honest.
  The climate says: *"It's okay to be yourself and be spontaneous."*

- **Absence of Stress ...** freedom from criticism, comparison, competition, and from value judgments.
  The climate says: *"Your ideas have precedence over mechanics. Your wild imaginings and daydreams are respected and prized."*

- **Seriousness ...** about the hard work and discipline involved, about the balance between the **freedom** to experiment with ideas and the **discipline** of making changes to produce a clear, precise final copy in language that communicates.
  The climate says: *"Writing is fun, but it also takes work."*

- **A Bottomless Barrel of Stimulation ...** loads of fresh ideas.
  The climate says: *"Your inner and outer worlds are full of thoughts and people and feelings and happenings that are worthy subjects for writing."*

You don't just walk in the first day of school and say, *"Look kids, I'm a nice person—you can trust me. You can express yourself freely."* The climate where kids will dare to write takes time to build. It's a little bit like love ... you don't convince someone you love her or him by saying it over and over. It takes months, sometimes years, of behaving in loving ways for you to be believed.

There are some steps teachers can take, however, to hasten the development of a comfortable home for writing growth. You can...

- **Share your own excitement about writing.** Your eagerness (and your enjoyment of your own writing) will spark theirs.

- **Respect the written word.** Share and enjoy freely all kinds of literature with kids, including stuff YOU write.

- **Remove obstacles to writing.** Competition, comparison, judgement, restrictive or dull forms or rhymes, over-analysis, and irrelevant or contrived assignments often choke out fluent writing.

- **Encourage carefree inventiveness.** A person can't create a brand new thing unless he/she feels free to do something nobody expects.

- **Provide plenty of time.** Writers need time for thinking, writing, trying, re-writing, changing, sharing. Many of the freshest thoughts appear after toying with several.

- **Let them write without stopping to correct.** Good ideas come faster than you can write—and you can rarely re-capture one once it's lost. You can ALWAYS go back and edit or fix.

- **Write together ... OFTEN.** Collaborative writing keeps the momentum going, eases discomfort for reluctant writers, shares good ideas, and teaches good writing skills.

- **Provide directions that challenge.** Don't be afraid to suggest a direction. All of us need that from time to time. Just make sure that you choose something that matters to kids.

- **Always make a way to share writing.** The importance you attach to their writing is the importance they'll give to theirs and others'.

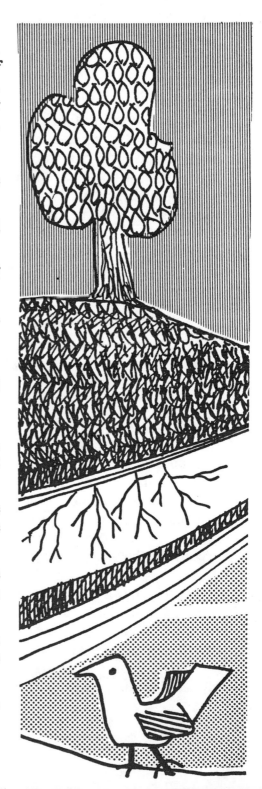

TAKE ANOTHER LOOK AT WRITING

When you hear *"writing in the classroom,"* what comes to mind? For too long, I thought of writing in pretty narrow terms. In the years I taught elementary grades, my repertoire was limited to stories, short poetry forms, and paragraphs—maybe with a myth or tall tale, an argument or a few essays sprinkled in once or twice a year. When teaching high school, I'd say essays won the prize for the over-worked genre in Mrs. Frank's English classes.

BIAS #6
WRITING IS BIGGER THAN YOU THINK

"Writing" is NOT synonymous with "stories" or "essays" or "themes." There are dozens of kinds of literature and writing forms—some long, some very short, some simple, some complex—which kids should hear, read, AND which they CAN write.

Thankfully, my limited world of writing has since opened up. Now I can see how very, very broad is this thing we call *writing*. It comes in hundreds of shapes, sizes, forms, topics, purposes, approaches, uses, and misuses. Writing is short, long, medium. It is serious, silly, heart-warming, tragic, irritating, fun, boring, simple, complex, imaginative, mundane, perplexing, satisfying, public, personal, private … all these things and many more. And kids need to be exposed to the whole realm of writing, not just a tiny corner of it.

One summer at a workshop, I asked a group of teachers to make a list of all of the kinds of writing they had done in the past two weeks. After a half-hour we sat back in awe at the length of the list and at the variety of necessary writing tasks involved in everyday living. (Incidentally, not one person listed *story* or *poem* or *essay* or several of the other things we assign all the time in school.)

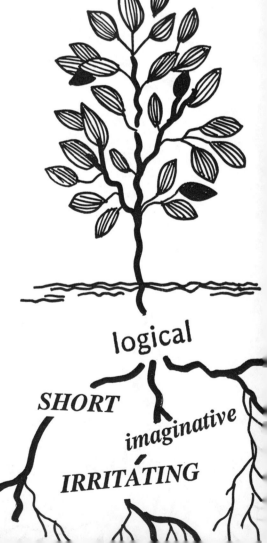

logical

SHORT

imaginative

IRRITATING

So I ask you to take another look at writing.

Right now...   **STOP...**

make a list of the kinds of writing you usually ask of your students or the forms you think they're able to write

THEN...

turn to the next page and look at the list of over two hundred kinds of forms that your students can try writing.

THEN...

... add your own ideas to the list.

... ask your students to expand the list.

... make a copy of those two pages and tape it to your desk.

... raise your right hand (or left hand) and vow to try at least thirty different kinds of writing during the school year. If your kids are too young to write this much or even to write at all, at least **expose** them to this great variety of kinds of writing.

I certainly hope that you won't drop story-writing or essay-writing from your classroom. But, the next time you think *writing,* please think in terms of ANY form of communication that involves the written word (or spoken word, for that matter).

And remember, you're teaching kids to LIVE—so include forms and topics that touch on a variety of the experiences of LIFE.

Simple   important   exciting   Distinctive

BORING   PUBLIC   SILLY   PRIVATE

TRAGIC   serious

OVER 200 ALTERNATIVES TO... *"Write A Story"*

lyrics

catalog entries

POST SCRIPTS

gags

dialogues

jingles

mistrakes

KOANS

EPITHETS

predictions

advertisements
advice columns
anecdotes
announcements
apologies
arguments
autobiographies
awards
ballads
bedtime stories
beginnings
billboards
biographies
book jackets
book reviews
bulletins
bumper stickers
campaign speeches
captions
cartoons
catalog entries
cereal boxes
certificates
character sketches
cinquains
codes
comic strips
comparisons
complaints
compliments
contracts
conversations
critiques

definitions
descriptions
dialogues
diamantes
diaries
diets
directions
directories
dramas
dreams
editorials
endings
epilogues
epitaphs
errors
essays
exaggerations
exclamations
explanations
fables
fairy tales
fantasies
folklore
fortunes
funny tales
game rules
good news-bad news
gossip
greeting cards
grocery lists
impromptu speeches
inquiries
interview questions

introductions
invitations
jingles
job applications
jokes
journals
legends
letters
lists
love notes
lyrics
magazine articles
memories
menus
metaphors
monologues
movie reviews
movie scripts
mysteries
myths
newscasts
newspapers
notebooks
nursery rhymes
observations
odes
opinions
pamphlets
parables
paragraphs
parodies
persuasions
phrases

plays
poems
post cards
post scripts
posters
predictions
problems
problem solutions
prologues
propaganda
proposals
protests
proverbs
puns
puppet shows
puzzles
questions
quips
quizzes
quotations
real estate notices
rebuttals
recipes
record covers
remedies
reports
requests
resumes
reviews
riddles
rhymes
sales pitches
satires

schedules
secrets
self descriptions
sentences
sequels
signs
silly sayings
skywriting messages
slogans
soliloquies
songs
song titles
speeches
spoofs
spooky stories
spoonerisms
sports analyses
sports reports
superstitions
TV commercials
TV guides
TV programs
tall tales
telegrams
telephone messages
thank you notes
theater programs
tips
titles
tongue twisters
traffic rules
travel brochures
travel logs

travel posters
tributes
trivia
view points
vignettes
want ads
wanted posters
warnings
wills
wise sayings
wishes
weather forecasts
weather reports
wonderful words
yarns
yellow pages

WRITE TO...

persuade
delight
convince
explain
surprise
confuse
clarify
describe
amuse
trigger imagination
expound
disturb
question
entertain

crossword puzzles
PARABLES
codes
malapropisms
answers
BLOOPERS
hymns
rhyMes
paragraphs
Prophecy

Children, there are words
pasted to the undersides of leaves
that match
your secrets.

                    Disorderly,
    full of dragons
and butterflies
        and sharks
pretending to be snowclouds
in September.
              Let the long beautiful ones hang
              off the edges of your paper.

And what if
you stuck them in store windows
with no price tags
            and put them on menus
            like specials

And what if
you stuck them into paper airplanes and sailed them
into India
or buried them under the begonias

And what if
you got up a parade
with some people playing cash registers
and everybody singing the poets' National Anthem

and making up their own
veined words.

                        Daniel Lusk

2

The FOUNDATION

"But they groan when it's time for writing!"

Bringing Kids Back To Language
Word Play Is NOT Just For Children
Language Delight And Classroom Life
Easing Into Writing
How To Use These Word-Play Ideas
How To Adapt An Idea To Your Writers
50 Ways To Build With Words

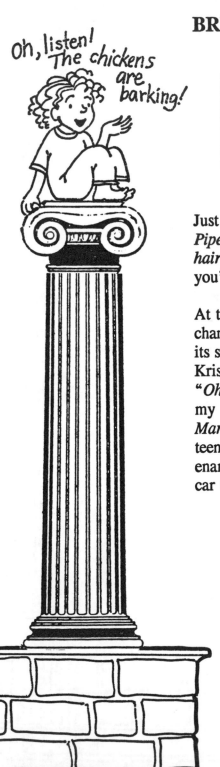

Oh, listen! The chickens are barking!

> ## BIAS #7
> ## LOVE OF LANGUAGE IS INBORN
>
> *The sounds and rhythms and melodies of words are pleasing to young minds and ears. From birth, children respond with delight to language.*

Just watch a group of young children enjoying the alliteration of *Peter Piper picked a peck of pickled peppers*, or the rhythm of *not by the hair of your chinny-chin-chin*, or the rhyme of *fox in socks*, and you'll be assured of the natural appeal of language.

At two years old, my neighbor Scotty used to march about my yard chanting his favorite phrase—*zucchini tetrazinni*—experimenting with its sound at various pitches and paces. I remember my toddler niece, Krista, exclaiming on the first morning we had our new chickens, *"Oh, listen! The chickens are barking,"* and explaining, when she saw my husband coming up the driveway on crutches, *"Look, Aunt Marge, Uncle Doug is swinging on wishbones!"* And when my now-teenage daughter, Sara, first learned to say *water tower*, she was so enamored with the words that she gleefully sang them one day on a car trip most of the way from San Francisco to Oregon.

> ## BIAS #8
> ## CHILDREN ARE FULL OF POETRY
>
> *Children's minds (even very young ones) create beautiful and sensitive combinations of words. In their efforts to explain their ever-new world with limited vocabularies, they often speak in complex metaphors and paint exquisite images.*

Smashed Potatoes by Jane Martel is a delightful collection of recipes created by children too young to write. These were dictated to an adult who transcribed them without alteration. And they are filled with many surprising, wonderful phrases such as...

Use red meatballs and the soapy kind of cheese that tastes a little bit rotten.

Mix the sauce in a blender so your elbows don't hurt.

Put every single thing you have in a mother-size pan...

Fringe up the lettuce in little heaps in all the bowls.

Put them in a skillet pan on the biggest black circle on the roof of your stove.

A four-year old who doesn't know the word *burner* describes this item as *"the biggest black circle on the roof of your stove."* But alas, by fourth grade, she knows the word and is unlikely to explain the concept with such color and visual appeal. So we try to help her forget *burner* and express the idea in a fresh way. If only we could keep her young-child metaphors flowing AFTER she enters school!

As you begin a chapter on the foundations of writing, I urge you to BELIEVE that inner poetry exists—that a love of language is NATURAL to children of all ages. So many times when I begin to write with kids, I'm holding on to expectations far too low, because I forget just that. Watching and listening to young authors such as those who wrote recipes in *Smashed Potatoes* helps me to keep sight of their natural poetry and of the real possibilities for kids and words.

I don't believe you have to teach your students to love language. But, you may have to BRING THEM BACK to words—especially if they are no longer young and free with expression. By taking advantage of their natural fascination with words, you CAN help to bring alive that pleasure—and turn it into a creative force. This chapter of exercises with words and short writing experiences will help you do just that—enjoyably.

WORD PLAY IS NOT JUST FOR CHILDREN

Words have so many surprising talents!

... Some amaze and excite and enchant you.
... Some frighten or anger or disappoint.
... Others convince you or make you doubt.

... Some words make you think of far-away places.
... Some remind you of home.
... Others take you to lands and spaces that don't even exist.

... Some words set up wonderful vibrations in your ears.
... Some conjure up enticing smells or make your skin crawl.
... Others feel absolutely delicious on your tongue.

I am a word-lover. I am fascinated by the POWER of words. And I believe kids should have loads and loads of experiences with the wonder and magic of words. Just as young bodies (and older bodies) are developed by physical play, so young minds (and older minds) are strengthened by verbal play.

And since words are the BASE UNITS of verbal expression, frolic with them serves as an important foundation to writing in any form.

I LOVE TO PLAY WITH WORDS

Words ❤ HAVE POWER

BIAS #9
EVERYBODY NEEDS TO PLAY WITH WORDS

Word play should never end. ALL writers—young, old, new, experienced, enthusiastic, lazy, struggling, gifted—need to go back and romp with words: to keep alive the appreciation of language, to freshen expression, to learn new words, to use old words in new ways, to stretch thinking, to strengthen the foundation of writing.

You may be thinking that the word-play and short writing ideas such as those in this chapter are just for young writers or beginning writers or slow writers or reluctant writers. OR you might see them as pre-writing exercises only useful to get students started on writing. OR you may think fooling around with words is only to build students up for writing longer pieces—the *real* stuff.

NOT SO! These are REAL WRITING. Who says writing has to be long to be **real**? The goal of writing instruction is not to be able to write lengthy pieces. The goal is to be able to write well. Short writing is for ALL writers .. and all should do it often. Surely, new writers, reluctant writers, very young writers will need lots of word play. But even advanced writers (including YOU) need to return often to such activities to expand and deepen use of words, to experiment with new forms, to keep enjoying language, and to improve writing.

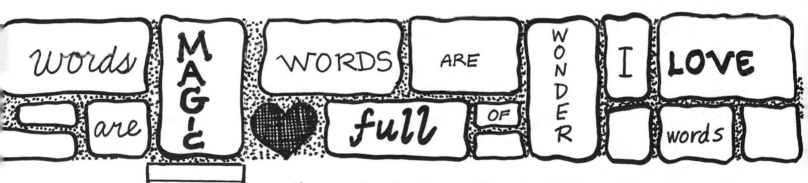

If you can't write short stuff, you probably won't be able to write long stuff. Kids who love words—who are comfortable with creating and rearranging phrases or sentences ... who gain confidence at writing short pieces—these are the writers that will have success with many kinds of writing, long and short.

Don't forget that the foundation of any structure needs to be kept strong. Don't get too deep into writing elaborate stories and essays and expository pieces to pay attention to sharpening word skills. Don't get too busy to remember: **WORDS are, after all, the major building blocks of written communication.**

LANGUAGE DELIGHT and CLASSROOM LIFE

So how can you turn kids back into word-lovers?

How can you help them keep their natural fascination with language?

How can you supply them with the building blocks of good writing?

You can tuck *poetic experiences* into any number of the scores of corners and crannies available in every school day—at **all** grade levels right up through high school and beyond. By *poetic experiences*, I mean games and happenings and small influences that act as living examples of the surprises, power, and joys in language.

I believe that a playful but serious language-loving teacher can be constantly and subtly building vocabularies, stretching imaginations, strengthening usage skills, and fertilizing enthusiasm for language.

Get in the habit of watching for possible places and ways to do this during each school day. Here are A DOZEN examples of the many possibilities that take only minutes. Start with these ... then add more.

1. When you check attendance or take lunch count, do it in poetry:
   Good morning, Tom—I'd like to say,
   It's cool to have you back today.

   You look tired, Sue—But that's all right,
   I didn't get much sleep either last night.

2. During a spelling test, instead of:

   The man put <u>oil</u> in his car's engine.

   use such colorful sentences as:

   Slimy <u>oil</u> oozed across the sizzling sidewalk and slithered silently over the curb.

THE BUIDING BLOCKS OF GOOD WRITING

Do it with Poetry

PLAY RHYME GAMES

Fuss over words

shattered
fractured
broken
split
splintered
demolished
fragmented
breach
rupture
snapped like a toothpick
crumbled to powder
fissure
chipped

The Fighting Olympians Break Down the Spartan Sports—

The Goths Fracture the centurions

3. Use those extra standing-in-line or calming-down or waiting-for-the-bell moments to finish a limerick, brainstorm synonyms, make up couplets, gather lists of rhyming words, play rhyme games with names, create sentences with homonyms, etc.

What word could you put with each of these to form a compound word or familiar phrase?

   child   bird   storm   surgery   wave   *(answer: brain)*

OR... *add the second line to this couplet:*

   In the last ten seconds before the sixth period bell...

OR... *Let's think of 7 things that could be done with a trunk.*

4. Hang up challengers around the room. For example:

Next to a poem, write: *Bet you can't learn this by Thursday!*

OR... beside a graffiti mural of superlatives: *Can you add two?*

OR... above a **How Many Ways to Say Win?** poster: *How many different ways can we say that one team won over another team?*

Vikings Conquer Trojans 21-13   **Tigers Devour Raiders**
Cavemen Blown Away by Tornado   **Grizzlies Maul Roseburg**

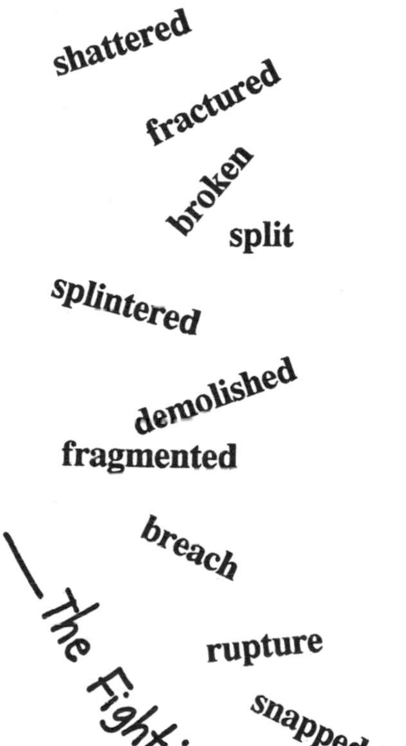

39

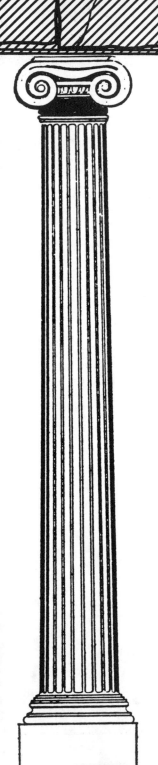

5. YOU bring in a *Word I'm Crazy About* (maybe every day or once a week). Teach it to the kids, then use it many times throughout that day.

*If this noise doesn't **abate**, I just may start screaming.*

*Tom, that's a fine **repartee**!*

*Now that's a **hyperbolic** statement if I ever heard one.*

*There seems to have been some **laxity** regarding this assignment.*

6. OFTEN—stop and fuss over words and special combinations of words that you come across when reading a story or working from a textbook or any other classroom material...

*Ahhh—PARABOLA ... now doesn't that word feel bubbly in your mouth? Can't you just envision that word tumbling out of the mouth of a big-mouthed fish? Tammy, would you get out the word book and add that to the page of **Words To Say When Your Mouth Is Full**?*

7. Trade a word each week with another class. When your class gets its word, make a big deal out of it. Ask that each person in the class use it 10 times during the week. Then do something spectacular with it ... build a painting around it, make a huge show-off poster, make it a title for an impromptu drama, create an acrostic with it, create a poem around it, etc. Make sure you share the spectacular new creation with the other class.

8. Listen to music together. Song lyrics often use words in creative combinations. You might suggest that your students add verses of their own ... or substitute different words and phrases ... or create their own lyrics ... or invent new titles.

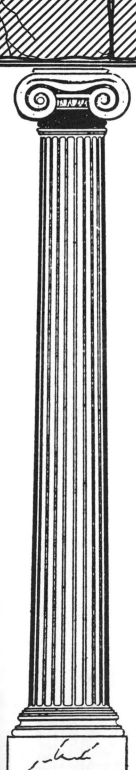

9. YOU memorize and burst into a poem or riddle or a pun—spontaneously—and often! When the day or period needs livening, that's the time for you to start in...

Once, I didn't mean to, but that was that...
I yawned in the sunshine and swallowed a gnat.

OR

Why aren't elephants allowed on beaches?
(Answer: ... because they're always letting their trunks down.)

10. Practice listening for the magic of words. Be on the lookout for pleasing or surprising combinations of words. Ask kids to bring one for tomorrow's homework or find one in the library or cut one from a magazine ... combinations such as...

... in the fern-deep grove at the midnight end of the garden.

11. Do lots of poetry together. Listen to it, memorize it, share it, march to it, set it to music, illustrate it, chant it, speak it in choirs, and have a Poetry Celebration. Then invite some others to hear the poems you've learned.

12. Send kids searching for phrases that create pictures in their minds. Then use torn paper shapes, clay, paint, ink, crayon or another medium to reproduce the images. Display the visual art along with the words...

... a slice of slivered moon in a green sky

... slow motion hot fudge sliding down mountains of golden vanilla ice cream

EASING INTO WRITING

Even confident writers sometimes feel the pangs of discomfort at the sound of, *"Write a..."* Here are some tips to help ease those pangs and help writers get started comfortably:

> ### BIAS #10
> ### WHAT YOU CAN SAY, YOU CAN WRITE
> *Creative talking is a stimulus to creative writing. Start with what kids say, then use that to convince them that they DO have something to write.*

* GET KIDS TALKING ... and TALK A LOT...

    Talk about questions or dreams or schemes or people or sounds or wild inventions or issues or feelings ... or anything!

    If a student thinks she CAN'T write, start with what she CAN do. Often the CAN is speaking. Therefore, many of the activities in this chapter are **oral** experiences designed to get ideas and communication flowing and to build the *I CAN* feeling.

, BE CAREFUL NOT TO CHOKE OFF EXPRESSION.

    It's awfully easy for kids' expression to be stifled or their thinking to be limited just by the way the teacher responds to their ideas or presents the assignment. Sometimes we say too much or give so many examples of one kind that our students hear the message, *"This is what the teacher wants,"* or *"This is the right way to think about this,"* instead of, *"What are all the possibilities?"* Begin these word-play activities in ways that leave open options for many directions.

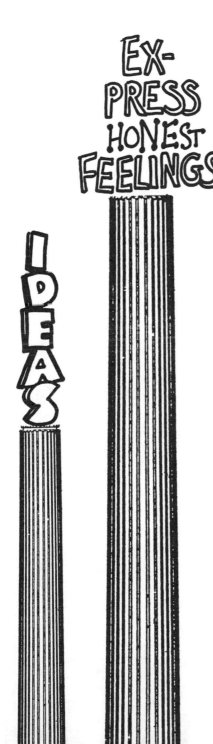

- **EXPRESS YOURSELF ... FREELY.**

The teacher makes A LOT of difference when it comes to getting kids comfortable with their own expression. I don't think I can emphasize this truth enough! Talk about your own wild ideas. Make public your fondest memories, your secret wishes, your haunting fears, your embarrassing moments (choosing content that's appropriate for your students to hear). A teacher's honesty is a very effective opener for students' bottled up notions and feelings. When you use the exercises in this chapter, make sure YOU contribute your ideas too. Of course, take care to offer your ideas in a way that doesn't make them seem right or superior to students' contributions.

- **START WITH SHORT, FUN, NON-THREATENING BITS OF WRITING.** This chapter is full of them.

By SHORT ... I mean exercises that fit into small segments of time and end without being over-worked or dragged on until someone gets bored.

By FUN ... I mean writing with strong kid-appeal: suggestions that challenge thinking, move along snappily, get them involved immediately, and capitalize on the natural attractions to words.

By NON-THREATENING ... I mean tasks that assure success for every writer or that sneak kids into writing without the fearful anticipation of a formal writing assignment.

Short Bits Of Writing

HOW TO USE THESE WORD-PLAY IDEAS

As you choose activities from the remaining pages of this chapter, keep in mind that they may be used in a variety of ways to meet a variety of needs. In most cases, you can use one of these ideas...

... during a 5-10 minute time slot
OR ... for a full writing period

... orally, with everyone contributing ideas
OR ... in writing, with students recording the lists, words, etc.
OR ... some of each within one lesson

... together, in collaboration
OR ... in small groups, as partners, in trios
OR ... alone, as an individual task

... just one time as a review or a motivator
OR ... repeated a few times throughout the year, adding depth and complexity (or a new twist) each time

... as it is
OR ... with adaptation (simplified or elaborated to fit your students) (*See "How to Adapt An Idea," on the next page.*)

... as a short experience
OR ... as the basis for a longer writing assignment

For example: Return to the impressions, ideas, phrases, and words collected in your WORD TASTING PARTY (page 51). Use these as raw material for poems, menus, food critiques, descriptive essays, etc.

HOW TO ADAPT AN IDEA TO YOUR WRITERS

Often teachers look at an activity and say, *"Oh, that's not the right level for my kids!"* Most good ideas can be adapted to many ages, abilities, or purposes, by varying...

... the topic you choose to focus on
... the simplicity or complexity of the words you use
... the number of examples required
... the duration of the exercise
... the depth to which the activity is developed
... the amount of assistance from teacher and peers
... the amount of direction given
... the extending exercises suggested
... the teacher's expectations
... the amount of writing involved

IT'S TREE-MENDOUS (from page 55), may be adapted like this:

for non-writers	Each student in the circle gives one word or idea related to *tree*. Keep going around the circle until the ideas stop flowing. (Maybe write a list of ideas for later use.)
for young writers	Same as above, only move on to other topics in small groups. Keep a list for one of the topics and ask students to write one sentence using at least four of the words.
for older writers	Have students work in pairs for 5 minutes to collect (in writing) a brainstormed list of words/ideas on a topic. Then give another 5 minutes to create a new list **on the same topic**, using **none** of the words from the first list.
for gifted writers	Fill a chalkboard or poster with as many words or 2-word phrases as possible related to a topic (ie: a football game). Set a limit on time for this. Then ask students to write a one-paragraph description of the experience of being at a football game **without using any of the words they've collected**. This forces the brainstorming process to continue and students to generate really fresh ideas.

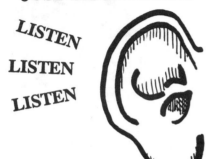

JUST LISTEN..........

LISTEN

LISTEN

LISTEN

LISTEN for interesting, unusual, beautiful or catchy words. Say them over and over. Gather and save words...**just for their sounds!**

abracadabra	ghosts	lazy	tremulous	chasm
giggle	whoosh	provocative	cinnamon	meander
gypsy	quince	goggles	buzz	haberdasher
grumble	cornucopia	caterpillar	eucalyptus	ephinany
slippery	trickery	murmur	labyrinth	corduroy
sassafras	sesame	sultry	sycamore	sophomore
shiver	marshmallow	ginger	enunciate	guzzle
galoshes	sneezes	gazebo	pirouette	gnash
smithereens	bamboozle	frangipani	blob	dollop

50 WAYS TO BUILD WITH WORDS

.........................THEN COLLECT!

Build lists of words for special purposes. These can be started in spare moments—then added to as the year goes along. NEXT, start a class word book. Every classroom needs one. Include a page for each category of words, for instance:

music words	city words	country words	irritating words
loud words	soft words	gentle words	soothing words
outdoor words	grumpy words	color words	future words
wet words	odd words	busy words	unbelievable words
public words	private words	tasting words	words you can move to
harsh words	indoor words	joyful words	slippery words
bewitching words	dry words	astonishing words	silly words
lazy words	convincing words	hurried words	dreamy words
serious words	frivolous words	conceited words	great-sounding words

The kinds of words you collect will depend upon the needs of your group. Use the collections again and again as raw material for writing during the year. For example:

When Julie gets stuck for ideas for her character sketch, she can get the people words page. OR... when Tim needs some specific words for his tale set in a city, he can take the city words page to his desk.

WORD WHEELS

In the hub of a cardboard wheel, write a word which is over-used in students' writing (*pretty, said, scary, person, ate, went, etc.*). Fill the spokes of the wheel with other ways of saying the word. THEN... post the wheels on a wall or tack them flat on the ceiling. You'll have a permanent **thesaurus-at-a-glance** for your writers all year long!

WORDS CAN MAKE YOU SICK

Think of words that, when you say them, might make someone feel:

frightened	*angry*	*sick*	*thirsty*	*jealous*
cold	*warm*	*nervous*	*wet*	*proud*
lazy	*sad*	*worried*	*in a hurry*	*suspicious*
surprised	*silly*	*slow*	*hungry*	*confused*

START WITH 25

As a group, compile a list of 25 words that students like—ANY words! Encourage ALL students to contribute. The words will vary with ages and interests of students. Here is a sample list:

aqua	*snooze*	*cinnamon*	*garbage*	*enchilada*
icicle	*scratching*	*abracadabra*	*crutches*	*purple*
slippery	*buttery*	*sunset*	*astonishing*	*surgeon*
explodes	*applesauce*	*shadows*	*awkwardly*	*slurp*
drooping	*polka-dotted*	*giraffe*	*slinking*	*eyelids*

Then, ask each to combine any 3 (or more) words into a phrase. They may later combine these short phrases into longer phrases and sentences. For example:

- *enchiladas on crutches! astonishing!*
- *a buttery, cinnamon sunset*
- *cinnamon applesauce explodes*
- *At sunset, shadows snooze.*
- *slippery, slinking garbage*
- *astonishing polka-dotted applesauce*
- *purple shadows drooping*
- *weary surgeon's drooping purple eyelids*
- *abracadabra! an aqua icicle!*
- *scratching, squirting shadows*
- *The giraffe's neck is a polka-dotted icicle.*
- *crutches slippery as icicles*
- *surgeon scratching through garbage*
- *awkwardly slurping enchiladas at sunset*

PALINDROMES

Some words read the same forwards and backwards:

pop	mom	noon	rotor	level	gag	bob
tot	nun	pup	refer	kayak	dad	wow

Phrases and sentences can be palindromes, too. Try to create some. It will take some creative thinking!

evil olive   *not a ton*   *too hot to hoot*
wet stew   *a toyota*   *pot top*
Sue us.   *No, son!*   *Ma! I Am!*
Was it a cat I saw?   *Madam, I'm Adam!*

WORD CAMPAIGNS

Promote words as contestants in a major election or contest. Kids can compose posters, banners, slogans, buttons, and speeches to convince others to vote for their words. Put words on posters and parade around the school promoting and showing off your words. You can even visit other classes and ask them to vote for their favorites.

THE GAME OF THE NAME

For each letter of your name write a word that is part of a newspaper headline, a story title, or advertising sign:

Sophomore Athlete Rejects Alabama

Martian Astronaut Rejects Greasy Eggs

Beware Eccentric Violinist!

Alligators Never Need Education

BABY TEETH ARE DROP-OUTS

Share some puns with students. Let them create their own or collect them from other sources. Keep a PUN notebook, hang them on a clothesline, or fill a graffiti mural with them.

A nervous mosquito is a jitterbug.
Gravity will let you down.
A talking dog is smarter than a spelling bee.
Custer wore Arrow Shirts!
Radar cops study speed reading.
Sorry, potatoes don't appeal to me.

SASSY SARAH

Create alliterative sentences by starting every word with the same sound. Pass one around a circle, with each student adding a word. Or, let kids make up their own. Keep the dictionaries handy for finding words.

Sam sifted sand in Suzie's sneakers.
Clumsy, cross camels created creamed croutons.
Melanie's music mostly makes mom mad.
Greedily, Gayle gobbled globs of greasy gravy.
Sassy Sarah, sitting sideways, sipped sodas and cited sixteen silly stanzas.
Tim tatoos Tom's ticklish tummy.

CONVERSATION STOPPERS

Think of sentences which, if said at the dinner table, would be guaranteed to stop the conversation and make people listen:

Mom, did you tell dad what you did to the car?

I wonder if Jimmy ever got out of that hole?

Dad, what's internal revenue? The man who called today said he was from there.

MAIL-A-WHALE?

Where would you mail a whale?
Don't ask your date to wait.
Here's a letter my goat wrote.
I'd like to see a possum blossom.
Don't ever shake a rake at a snake.
Should you jump rope with the pope?
Never get in a canoe with a gnu.
Would you go out after dark with a shark?

These are a challenge for older kids—and great fun for little kids. Make up some of your own, and add hilarious, inviting illustrations.

TEAKETTLE

Teakettle is a word game my mom taught me when I was very young. Get an old teapot, and let kids fill it with pairs of homophones. When there's a spare moment, kids can take turns drawing a pair from the teakettle and making up *teakettle* sentences ... sentences where two or more homophones are replaced by the word *teakettle*. Others try to figure out what the homophones are.

I teakettle an ocean liner sailing on the blue teakettle. (see...sea)

The king had teakettled ten years when he met his demise one teakettly night by letting go of the teakettles on his swift-moving horse. (reign...rain...rein)

IDIOMS DRIVE ME CRAZY

Start a list of idioms:

I'm tickled pink.
She has a frog in her throat.
We had the minister for lunch.
If you break that, I'll crown you!
You're driving me up the wall!

Get your students to listen for them at home, on TV, in school...anywhere. Start making up your own, too.

MY DENTIST BORES ME TO TEARS

Try to hold a conversation full of *occupational puns:*

By gum, I hear you went to the dentist today.
Yes, it was quite a filling experience.
Did you meet the new hygienist, named Floss?
Definitely-I found her to be captivating!
It's a drain on our budget to hire a plumber.
Mom's hair dresser keeps on the cutting edge of her profession.
That policewoman has an arresting smile.

WHAT'S OUR BAG?

Take turns putting *secret* objects into a bag. Each student peeks into the bag, then writes a related word on the bag. Later, use the bags with their word lists for writing *What Am I?* riddles.

OR

Classmates can try to guess what's in the bag after someone orally supplies words as clues. But they may guess only by asking if other words apply. For instance, *Is it buoyant? Does it inflate? Would it deteriorate after a few weeks? Could it be emerald in color?*

YOU NAME IT!

Did you hear about the plumber named **Seymour Pipes** and his partner **Duane A. Tubb**? Or the opthamologist named **Benjamin I. Ball**? Or the barber named **Harry Locks**? Or the baker, **Joe Dough**? My sister-in-law has gone for oral surgery to **Dr. Slaughter** and a friend insists he used to live next door to a mortician named **I.C. Stiphs**. (Do you believe that one?) Anyway, it's fun and brain-stretching to make up names for persons or animals. What would you name:

an elephant?.....twins?.....a huge dog?.....a clown?.....a telephone repair person?.....a skydiver?..... an exterminator?.....a tree surgeon?.....a crossing guard.....a foot doctor.....a doughnut maker?

I've seen a fabric shop called **Nip and Tuck** and a pet store named **Feathers and Fins** and a combination clock and beauty shop called **Locks and Clocks** (or was it a combination clock shop—detective agency called **Crime Time**?). Ask your students to name business establishments such as:

a waffle house.....a water bed store.....a heart surgeon's office.....a wig boutique.....a rock shop..... a washing machine repair service.....a music store.....a parachute shop.....a mattress store.....a plastic surgeon.....a barber shop and a pizza shop sharing one store....a combination butcher and accountant.... a foot doctor....a yo-yo shop....a tire shop sharing space with an orange juice bar....a hot tub store

BLOOPERS

Also known as *spoonerisms*, these are mixed-up phrases such as:

Pardon me, miss, your ship is slowing.
Who milled the spilk?
I want creaches and peam on my cereal.

Make some bloopers of your own. Ask your kids to try whole paragraphs full of bloopers.

P.S. I'm not as dumb as some thinkle peep I am!

VERBAL GYMNASTICS

Choose some words or short phrases with differing rhythms. Have kids march or drum or stretch to the rhythm of each word. Try:

elevator operator
elephantiasis
banana, banana, banana
wiggle, wiggle, wobble, waddle
bother, bamboozle, bedazzle
thump, bump, clump, stump
metamorphosis
intensity, density, dentistry
lugubrious
indescribably, indubitably immense

Go on to longer sentences. Ask individuals or groups to make up movements to fit the rhythms-and teach them to the class.

WHAT'S MISSING?

Find the word that completes the othe each group:

roar	stairs	set	seven	*up*
ward	side	ache	quarter	*back*
horse	ball	gad	swatter	*fly*
cake	cloth	blue	cottage	*cheese*
way	post	water	garden	*gate*
goose	first	town	stairs	*down*
mate	friend	shape	member	*ship*
gold	pan	storm	mop	*dust*
hum	ear	corps	beat	*drum*
nail	tom	green	tack	*thumb*
stone	shine	blue	harvest	*moon*
time	check	doors	side	*out*

Get kids involved in making up the examples—finding 4 words with another word in common.

WORD TASTING

About mid-way through the morning, give each student an apple (or celery, carrots, granola). Ask them to say or write a word as you direct:

Write a word that tells something about how your apple looks.
Write a word that tells about how your apple feels.
Take a bite. Write a sound word. How does it sound when you bite in?
Write a word that tells how it feels in your mouth.
Write a taste word.
Write a word that tells how it feels when you swallow.
Write an after-taste word.
Finish: The girl next to me chewing on her apple sounds like...
    Eating apples reminds me of...
    This apple is as crunchy as...
    This apple drips like...
    I'd rather eat apples than...
Can you think of a person who reminds you of an apple?
    Write: _____ is like an apple because...

51

RdiNVENTAMeaNiNG

WOULD A LAPIDARY PLAY LEAPFROG IN A LYCEUM?

A dictionary exercise that teaches words in a way kids will remember!

1. Could a GARGOYLE gargle?
2. Are you PARSIMONIOUS?
3. Do you like your PHYSIOGNOMY?
4. Where does a COWLICK reside?
5. Would you climb into a MAW?
6. Does a waffle have a WATTLE?
7. Would a BARNACLE wear a MONOCLE?
8. Name two things that are MUCILAGINOUS.
9. Would you ask a GAMMON to dance with you?
10. Is the fat lady at the circus likely to be SVELTE?
11. Do you know anyone who is FASTIDIOUS?
12. Could you put ice cream into a CALABASH?
13. Do you think an OBELISK would make a good pet?
14. How could a VECTOR be harmful to a RECTOR?
15. Would a LAPIDARY play leapfrog in a LYCEUM?
16. Would you expect to find a UVULA in an orchestra?
17. Is a boy's first violin lesson likely to be EUPHONIOUS?
18. If you're going to meet a TYCOON, would you take an umbrella?
19. Might you get arrested if you try to ABET a crime?
20. Which is more valuable to your mother, her SPATULA or her SCAPULA?
21. When was the last time you were accused of being OBSTREPEROUS?
22. Which is more SANGUINARY, a vampire or a VERANDA?

Have kids answer the questions. Better yet, have them make up the questions, researching words they don't know but think it would be good to learn.

DO-IT-YOURSELF WORDS

Have a session for creating original words. *Magniflubescent* isn't a real word—but it certainly should be! Kids can create words that are meaningful, useful and fun. Ask them to write their words in sentences, prepare dictionary entries, or make up synonyms.

DILLY DEFINITIONS

Give kids a word they do NOT know. Ask them to write a definition for it. (OR they may choose their own unknowns from a dictionary.) Then, enjoy sharing the new meanings before you compare them to the actual definitions. You might choose words that you want the students to be learning anyway. Try:

copacetic	quaggle	siluroid	verdant
tigon	termagant	garbulent	raucous
amok	stentorian	mome	pruinose
syllabub	sullied	commodius	surplice
zealot	felicity	ubiquitous	efficacious
cardoviar	druid	puissance	jollification

(Try some made-up words too!...I did)

inVEntAWordinVEntAmEaNingIn
vEntAWo
amean
.n gIn VE
invent

WORDS YOU'D LIKE TO KNOW

Present 4 or 5 new words to the class without giving the definitions. Or ask each student to choose a few unfamiliar words from the dictionary. (Don't read the definitions!) Use the words in a poem, saying, bit of advice, or sentence. Here are some finished examples done with unfamiliar words:

A DROLL came down with JABORANDI
Her fever rose, her DRUIDS sank low.
Dr. VERDANT arrived and prescribed SCRUPLES
And said, "You'll be well in a MEMENTO!"   Hilary, Grade 4

The frog croaked as he JADED from PLACID to PLACID
He stopped on a PROLOGUE to sip VERDANTLY from a pool of DIADEMS.
                Christopher, Grade 3

Don't CORNICE me with KISSES
While I'm dancing the MACABRE.   Jenny, Grade 2

ALPHABET ANTICS

For each letter of the alphabet, try to write a word that fits into a particular category you've chosen. For example:

Words That Describe Children

Adventuresome	Noisy
Busy	Obedient
Curious	Polite
Delightful	Quick
Eager	Rambunctious
Frivolous	Sneaky
Generous	Tireless
Horrible	Useful
Ingenious	Vocal
Joyful	Wonderful
Kind	X-tra special
Lovable	Young
Mischievous	Zesty

Names of Animals

Alligator	Nuthatch
Butterfly	Opossum
Camel	Porcupine
Dinosaur	Quail
Elephant	Rattlesnake
Fox	Spider
Gorilla	Tiger
Hyena	Unicorn
Iguana	Viper
Jackal	Wolf
Koala	Xiphosuran
Llama	Yak
Mole	Zebra

HEADLINERS

Create original titles for dances...or books...or magazines...or movies...or songs... or articles...or musical albums...or TV shows...or events.

What would you call...

    ... a new reader for first graders?
    ... a song to be sung at a Blueberry Festival?
    ... a banquet for zoo animals?
    ... a book on how to give a haircut?
    ... a new Halloween dance?
    ... a magazine for extra-terrestrial beings?
    ... an album by a singing motorcycle gang?
    ... a theme song for a queen's coronation?
    ... a movie about a mystery on the moon?

It's challenging to ask the questions, too. And it's valuable to work with just ONE idea for a while to see how many different titles can be invented.

Why did the milk shake?

It frightened her to see the butter-fly.

Why was the little shoe crying?

Because, his mommy was a loafer and his daddy was a sneaker.

Why did the roast beef blush?

Because he saw the salad dressing.

Can the bread box?

No, but the soup can.

What is Dracula's favorite place to hang out around New York City?

The Vampire State Building.

How is a lollipop different from a postage stamp?

One is a stick to lick, the other takes a lick to stick.

Why was the peach flirting?

Because she saw a banana who was appealing.

Why did the apple turnover?

Because he saw the jelly roll.

How can you tell the difference between a jeweler and a prison warden?

One sells watches, the other watches cells.

How is a letter different than a lady going to church?

One is addressed in an envelope, the other is enveloped in a dress.

SENTENCE STRETCHING

Start with a short sentence or group of words. Pass it around to about 6 people, with the rule that each person must add or change ONE word to make the sentence more specific and more interesting:

She ate dinner.

became, for some first graders:

A hungry ballerina gobbled her sloppy green soup.

Sixth graders turned it into:

A ravenous sow slurped down mush and slop with uncouth gulps.

IT'S TREE-MENDOUS!

With a partner, brainstorm all the words you can which are in any way related to trees. Allow the brainstorming to continue as long as ideas are flowing, then switch to a different topic. OR, collect the words you've shared and save them for a later writing exercise. As a teacher, you can encourage divergent thinking by contributing some words and ideas of your own to introduce other directions or possibilities.

wood...pencils...hollow...willow...forest... shade...sap...lightning...gnarled...seed... nest...petrified...paper...splinters... logging...family...swing...climbing... cones...leaves...deer... etc.

WHAT'S UP?

move UP	open UP	dress UP
light UP	close UP	fix UP
lock UP	wind UP	pull UP
wake UP	ante UP	UP on the news
UP to par	UP to it	fed UP
finish UP	UP to my ears	grow UP
beat UP	UP for election	clam UP
stir UP trouble	ring UP	put UP
chin UP	time's UP	shut UP
UP for robbery	speak UP	stopped UP
done UP	clogged UP	give UP
come UP	throw UP	clean UP
keep UP	rise UP	write UP

There are other words in our language that have this many uses (just look for the long dictionary entries): *time...run...down...over...under...side...set...back...* Start collecting a list of the many uses of a little word, then ask students to work in groups or as a whole group to combine the uses into a story or poem or paragraph. Here is an *OUT* story done by three fourth-graders.

You're OUTnumbered

For crying OUT loud, it sure is confusing trying to make sense OUT of all the ways to use the word OUT.

Before you're even OUT of diapers you learn that people can be OUT to lunch, start OUT on a trip, cry OUT with pain, dig OUT of a snowbank, turn OUT a cake, fade OUT of the picture, be OUT of style, give OUT compliments, back OUT of a deal, run OUT of money, behave OUT rageously, get Chinese food at a carry OUT, break OUT of jail, fake OUT other people, or dash OUT to the OUThouse.

When you first try to spin OUT on your tricycle and you wipe OUT—your mother can get OUT the dirt by washing it OUT or soaking it OUT or rubbing it OUT, and if none of those work, she can throw it OUT!

In school you find OUT fast not to get OUT of line. You're OUT of luck if you answer OUT of turn, because then the teacher won't let you OUT to recess until she bawls you OUT. And when you're OUT side playing softball, you hope you don't strike OUT. Don't get OUT of sorts with the umpire or you'll get kicked OUT.

When you grow up you learn that an OUT of sight chick is a knock OUT, and if she's OUT of your league, all you can do is eat your heart OUT. When you're old enough to go OUT on a date, you'll probably break OUT with pimples. You can take your date OUT to your favorite hang OUT—and if she doesn't want to make OUT, you'll feel down and OUT. Then you'll get OUT before you're left OUT in the cold.

Well, we're about OUT of our minds with this OUTlandish stuff, so we're going to cut OUT because we've run OUT........ Doug and Scott and Peter G.

WORD RUBBINGS

Cut some letters from cardboard or from any kind of textured material. Create word designs by placing paper over the letters and rubbing with charcoal, pencil, chalk, or dark crayon. Choose textures which match the unique flavor or meaning of this particular word.

WORD MOBILES

Hang some letters from wire mobiles to form a word...OR...combine several related words on one mobile...OR...hang several large letters on which you've written words that begin with that letter...OR...hang words that could be arranged into a story.

WORDS OF ART

Ask students to create a a design by repeating a word (or several words) in a pattern...OR...by varying sizes and shapes of letters within the word...OR...they can fill up the paper with one big, huge word which they've embellished.

WORD CHAINS

Create a chain of words that surrounds the classroom, climbs the walls, and encircles windows. Draw or write favorite words forever! BUT—the last letter of one word MUST BE the first letter of the word that follows it in the chain. How long can your chain get?

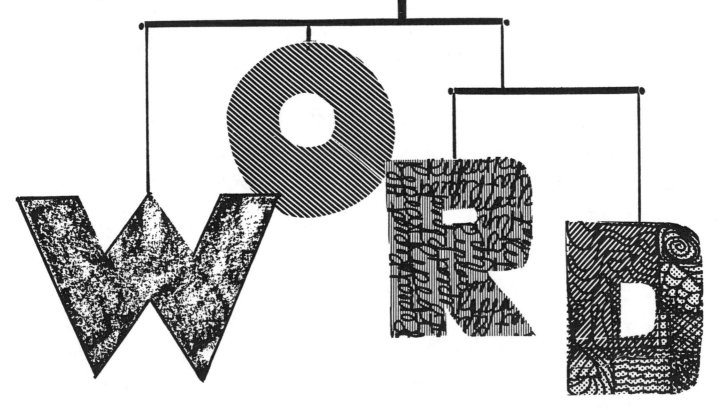

A WORD IS WORTH A THOUSAND PICTURES

BIG, BIG WORDS

Kids of all ages are fascinated by seeing and hearing really big words. This doesn't necessarily mean really *long* words. **BIG** can mean *unusual, sharp, loud, heavy, complicated, strong,* or *very important-sounding* words. There are many fascinating ones to look at, listen to, fool around with, and learn about. Try just saying some. Try to guess what they might mean. Write tales about them. Try to explain them to friends in a letter. Try to learn a few and use them often to impress people. Start with these, then use your dictionaries to find more:

moxie	*beriberi*
imbroglio	*parsimonious*
pandiculation	*gargoyle*
oxymoron	
lachrymose	
juxtapose	
zealot	
vicissitude	
paradox	
zabaglione	
bibliomania	
obsequious	
mucilaginous	
septuagenarian	
quixotic	
polyglot	
indubitable	
sousaphone	
glockenspiel	

Have fun creating short phrases that can be used as eye-catching bumper stickers. Kids will enjoy creating puns, outrageous sayings, and take-offs on other bumper stickers they see.

Rescue Raisins From Cereal

Broccoli Kills Brain Cells

SOCCER is a KICK

Give Blood-Play Football

OWLS GIVE A HOOT...!

HINK PINKS

A timeless favorite, these are pairs of rhyming words, an adjective followed by a noun (such as *firm worm* or *mellow jello*), called *hink pinks, hinky pinkies,* or *hinkety pinketies,* depending on the number of syllables.

Here are a few to start with. Let students try making up more. They'll need to create a clue to help others figure out the rhyming pair.

broader arachnid	*wider*	*spider*
nervous burglar	*shook*	*crook*
noisy mob	*loud*	*crowd*
blender repair person	*mixer*	*fixer*
evil preacher	*sinister*	*minister*

HIDE-A-WORD

The job of hiding a word in a piece of writing gets kids writing without pain. They concentrate so hard on making one word look inconspicuous, that they forget they're doing a writing task! Pass out *mystery words* for kids to hide in their writing.

Would you ever guess that I cracked three bones in my hand yesterday just because I wanted an ice cream cone so badly? The surgeon couldn't believe the story I told about how it happened. I should have let go of the ice cream cone and used both hands or my shoulder to stop the heavy door from crashing shut. But, alas! I decided to protect the luscious marble mocha fudge cone instead.

SO MANY QUESTIONS

A question is a short, yet important, piece of writing. Kids are full of questions. Formulating and writing questions gives kids of all ages a short, easy-success writing experience. Ask your students to think of questions they wish they could have answered. They can try for a list of 5, 10, or 20 questions, depending on the age and ability. Some kids' questions *(mixed ages):*

> *Do cats really have nine lives?*
> *Why do eyes blink?*
> *Are all mothers grouchy in the morning?*
> *Why do people have different shapes?*
> *Can a dog smile?*
> *Why doesn't it hurt to cut your hair when it hurts to cut your finger?*
> *Who decided school should last through 12th grade? Why not 10th or 15th?*
> *Does a rainbow actually have ends?*

MULTIPLE MEANINGS

Work together to make lists of words that have more than one meaning...words such as:

trunk...back...down...sign...quarter...train....

Have students make illustrated posters, stories, sentences, or riddles showing that they understand the multiple meanings of some of these words.

> ***The elephant got his trunk***
> ***tangled in his trunks when he***
> ***climbed on the trunk to get into the trunk.***

WRITE WITH REBUS

A *rebus* uses pictures or symbols to help communicate words or parts of words. Kids love to decipher and create words, phrases, sentences, conversations, advice, and sayings with rebus drawings. Try some!

FRAMED FAVORITES

Get everybody (including yourself) started on a personal word frame (frames brought from home or frames you've made). Begin filling them with your VERY FAVORITE WORDS. Do this for several days, then keep the frames and add words throughout the year. Use these words often as starters for writing experiences throughout the year. For example:

Use 6 of your words in a color poem...or...Use 3 of them in a joke.
Make a poster advertising one of the words for sale.
Write a speech telling what is fantastic about one of the words.
Make 4 of the words into a tongue twister.

WORDS ON THE MOVE

Below are some words for NOT standing still. Ask kids to move their bodies to show the meaning of each. (They don't have to <u>know</u> the meanings.)

wiggle wobble gyrate pirouette twist flop tremble shiver flutter scurry fluctuate amble gallop writhe leap strut swoop flail shuffle

Find other words for moving. Talk about the subtle differences among the meanings of the words.

WORD SCAVENGERS

Get kids learning new words by sending them on a scavenger hunt for words right in their own environments. To show that they know what the word means, they must bring an object to school that somehow shows the word. Look for such items or colors or textures as:

lozenge	vase	thesaurus
tumeric	jute	adhesive
syringe	wrench	chamois
baster	vise	coarse
mallet	matte	coaster
woven	khaki	alabaster

5 WORDS TO KEEP

Ask students which words in the world they would keep if they could only have 5. Take time for sharing the words and their reasons for keeping them. Later, ask them to write a phrase next to each word telling why they kept it. Doing this builds a poem!

BAMBOOZLE	*Sounds big and powerful*
YES	*I can! I will!*
CHOCOLATE	*Who'd be without it?*
SNOW	*Cold, white, friendly*
YOU	*I like having you around!*

GRAFFITI

CUSTER WORE ARROW SHIRTS

KICK the BUCKET

One Good Turnip Deserves Another!

Does anyone ever bark up the RIGHT tree?

A cow eating grass is a lawn mooer.

WEREWOLVES MOONLIGHT?

A baseball bat is a fly swatter

Mt. Eve Rest is lazy

"On the horns of a dilemma"

Take the

Why make no bones about it?
Why not make no livers about it?

Aunt Marge: *"Oh, kids, look at the full moon!"*

Krista, age 3:   *"What's it full of?"*

Scotty, age 2:   *"Does it have a zipper so you can fill it up?"*

3

The
ROMANCE

"They always say they can't think of anything to write."

What's Going On Here?
Starting Love Affairs With Ideas
Where Do Writers Get Ideas?
Romancing Writers
Which Romancers Are Right For Your Writers?

WHAT'S GOING ON HERE?

This morning some writing sessions are in progress around the Lincoln School District...

... John Ebel's eighth grade language arts students are building sculptures of wire, wood, styrofoam, foil, clay and other materials to express such themes as *Surprise, Rage, Change, Pride, Confusion, Discovery, Conflict, Contentment, Jealousy, Peace, Protest, Communication, Honesty, Hurt, Joy.*

... Maggie Boyle's fourth graders are blowing feathers in the air, then catching them on elbows, toes, noses, heads, knees.

... Students in Carl Reed's fifth-sixth grade are tasting dishes their families contributed to an international smorgasbord.

... Peggy Nicholson's third graders are eating peanut butter.

... Gina Wang's sophomores are all coming into English class wearing green—green shirts, hats, shoelaces, tatoos. Some have even painted their faces green. Others have tried out green hair.

... Jacob Walsh's second grade class is visiting a local cemetery.

... Kids in Angela Giavanni's special ed classroom are telling tales about their most frightening experiences.

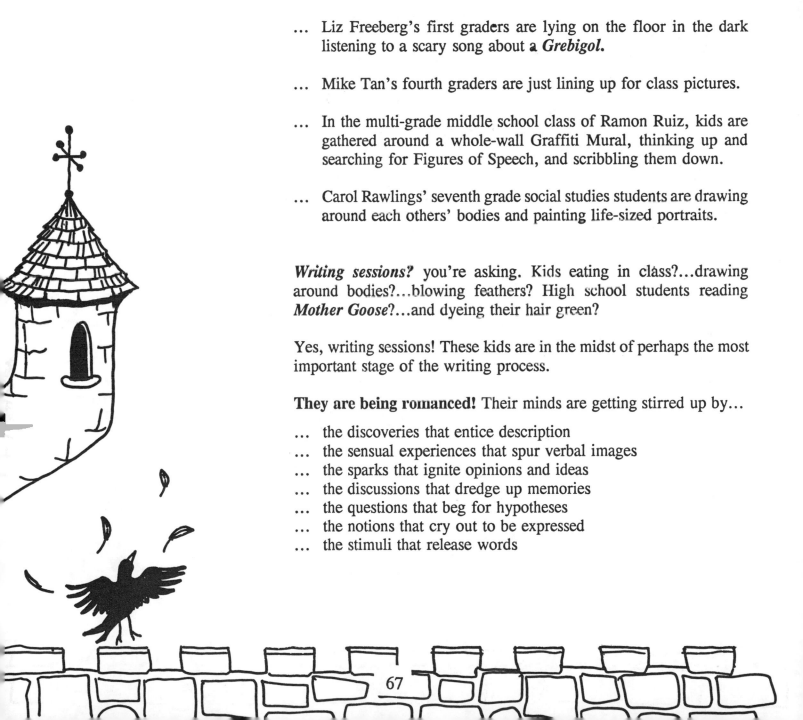

... The seniors in Tim Cislo's writing class are reading aloud to each other Mother Goose rhymes and Grimm's Fairy Tales.

... Liz Freeberg's first graders are lying on the floor in the dark listening to a scary song about a *Grebigol.*

... Mike Tan's fourth graders are just lining up for class pictures.

... In the multi-grade middle school class of Ramon Ruiz, kids are gathered around a whole-wall Graffiti Mural, thinking up and searching for Figures of Speech, and scribbling them down.

... Carol Rawlings' seventh grade social studies students are drawing around each others' bodies and painting life-sized portraits.

Writing sessions? you're asking. Kids eating in class?...drawing around bodies?...blowing feathers? High school students reading *Mother Goose*?...and dyeing their hair green?

Yes, writing sessions! These kids are in the midst of perhaps the most important stage of the writing process.

They are being romanced! Their minds are getting stirred up by...

... the discoveries that entice description
... the sensual experiences that spur verbal images
... the sparks that ignite opinions and ideas
... the discussions that dredge up memories
... the questions that beg for hypotheses
... the notions that cry out to be expressed
... the stimuli that release words

STARTING LOVE AFFAIRS WITH IDEAS

> **BIAS #11**
> **THE IN-PUT AFFECTS THE OUT-POUR**
>
> *Experiences are the catalysts that ignite expression. The hearing, enjoying, sharing, trying, discussing, remembering, doing, experimenting, discovering of life...flows into writing... NATURALLY.*

This has happened so often that I'm tempted to guarantee it for you: when I go into a classroom and get kids involved in a doing or talking experience, or when I start sharing literature with a special appeal—**KIDS ASK TO WRITE!** One day I visited a fifth grade, ready to read a cycle of *Warning* poems and start kids writing some warnings of their own. The teacher cautioned me that the class was *"rowdy and uncreative and never interested in writing,"* so I was ready with ten fun and motivating pieces. After just a few, kids were getting out pencils and paper, and one boy piped up, *"Hey, could you please stop now so we can write our own?"*

PLEASE, don't ask kids to write without giving them some input! It can be ongoing exposure to literature or any writing samples or yesterday's science experiment that flopped. It can be a piece of literature, an art activity, music, movement, talking, telling jokes. It can be small, short, big, long. But **something romantic** needs to precede the writing assignment: some happening that jars loose the words inside their heads and sets free a flow of ideas.

If you try this (as I did one April afternoon in my fourth grade)...

Okay, kids ... today is the first really nice spring day. Isn't it exciting to have the sunshine back after a long winter? Take out your paper and write a poem about spring. You have twenty minutes until recess, so get started quickly...

... probably most of them WILL write, (especially if they know they **have to** before they can go to recess). But you'll get things like this... (which you won't be happy with ... and neither will they)...

> I like spring   *(an actual result of the*
> The robins sing   *above assignment)*
> It is a nice thing.
> Ding-a-ling.
>   The End

The next spring, I tried some **romance:**

- We all moved outside with paper and pencils, some large pieces of posterboard, and a fat marker.

- For 15 minutes we lay on our backs in silence (well, as much silence as is possible from 25 fourth graders)—breathing the air, tasting the wind, watching and feeling spring.

- We dug our bare feet into the dirt ... rolled in the grass ... picked up bugs ... inspected tender buds ... felt the tree bark.

- Then, we gathered under a tree and made lists of sights and sounds and smells and feelings and tastes and sensations and experiences of spring on posterboard.

- With those lists on posterboard leaning against trees as our source of ideas and inspiration, we moved slightly apart from the others and wrote ... and wrote. I asked each to do at least two poems or short prose pieces. Some kids wrote ten.

Pieces such as these appeared, accompanied by proud smiles...

My principal wasn't sure about such outdoor expeditions— especially when neighbors called to ask, "Are you aware there is a teacher rolling down the hill in your school yard—what is going on over there?" So I learned to inform him ahead of time with educational goals in hand, invite him to join us, and show off our finished work. One year we even delivered to neighbors a news-flash bulletin to show off our poetry. We called it: **"Remember-the-day-you-saw-us-rolling-in-the-grass?"**

> *Spring comes.*
> *Worms wiggle.*
> *Flies bother.*
> *Bugs chase each other.*
> *Sunshine warms you.*
> *Teachers let kids outside.*
> *Spring comes.*
>   *Jonathan, Grade 4*

> *New mown grass smells prickle my nose,*
> *New-born flies whisper in my ears,*
> *Damp new dirt pets my bare feet,*
> *Fresh new air teases my tongue.*
> *A brand new spring brings*
>   *smiles to my heart.*
>   *Amy, Grade 4*

> *An ant crawled over my leg*
> *And back on to the grass.*
> *He didn't even care that I was here.*
>   *Tom, Grade 4*

WHERE DO WRITERS GET IDEAS?

Meanwhile, back in the classrooms:

Mr. Ebel's students have finished their sculptures. Now they are sculpting with words: creating written pieces which match the themes of their artwork... such as this attachment to a wire sculpture:

Tangled jealousy.
Inside you, it wraps and winds around your feelings
And cuts into you.
The tightening hurt twists and stabs
Like knotted wire
With sharp, jutting ends.

The feather-blowing fourth grade has moved into word collecting. And word collections are offering selections for lines in cinquains...

Feather	*Feather*
Fluffy, silky	*Airy, tickly*
Twirling, tumbling, floating	*Blowing, turning, twisting*
Soft as melted marshmallow	*Light as an empty eggshell*
Feather	*Fluff*

During the smorgasbord, students are writing tasty phrases to describe the entrees, for use when they create restaurant menus tomorrow...

soft, shimmery noodles
chewy red meat huddled in a smooth rice wrapper
crunchy with sweet peppers
moistness of tender beef tidbits against a brittle crunch of almonds
oily morsels of pork
slender celery fingers oozing with tart yogurt
a sauce of syrupy maple
chin-dripping firecracker tomato sauce
...with a blanket of the lightest lemon cream

The peanut butter eaters in Ms. Nicholson's third grade have gathered a long list of taste and texture words and another list of convincing sales slogans and are busy creating posters and ad layouts to sell various brands of peanut butter...

- *sticky as rubber cement*
- *smooth as warm taffy*
- *spreads like whipped cream*
- *creamy, butterscotchy brown*
- *crunchy surprise in a peanutty cream*
- *a spoonful of tasty energy*

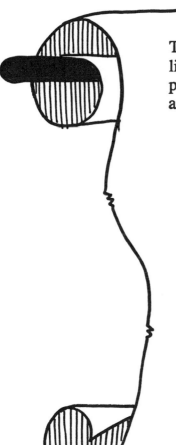

The sophomore English class, dressed in green, has gathered many lists of **green** ideas: **green** tastes, sounds, feelings, smells, sights, places, experiences. And they've put these ideas together into group and individual poems, such as...

Green is the rhythmic chirping of crickets,
The way a pickle pinches your tongue,
And the dentist's fluoride treatments.

Green is mold and jealousy.
And the velvet stretch of a golf course.
Green is having the flu in math class.

Green stains the seat of your baseball pants,
Paints a forest of pine trees,
Drips slime on a slippery frog,
Dots a pond with algae,
Lends the music to a rushing stream.

Quiet is green.
So is spinach, St. Patrick's Day, a lizard, and loneliness.
You are green when your heart is broken.

Green is sour.
Green is cold and crunchy.
You can take it to the bank.

At the cemetery, second graders are making up original epitaphs...

In this place lies Captain Hook
A pirate should have been a cook!

Mountain climber, Jenny McCheek
Chose a volcano as her target peak.

In Angela's special ed class, the *afraid* phrases have been gathered and arranged into a collaborative poem...

thump thump fear

When you're afraid,
Your hands get watery,
You feel cold all over,
And you want to hold something.
Your breathing changes
And your heart bangs in your ears,
And your stomach jumps around.
It's like being inside an ink-black closet.

In the senior writing class, students have read many fairy tales and Mother Goose rhymes. They've also read several news articles from local newspapers and gathered words and phrases used frequently in news stories. And they've gone on to report events from the fairy tales and nursery rhymes as if they were current events happening today by writing news articles with headlines such as...

Local First Grade Boy Wins Candle-Jumping Contest

Woodcutter Battles Wolf in Daring Rescue

Wolf-Burning Pigs Go To Trial

Politician Georgie Porgie Charged With Harrassment

The song about the Grebigol now has two verses added by the first graders caught in the spooky spirit of mysterious monsters...

The Grebigol has such terrible teeth
Nine up above and twelve beneath.
He growls and grunts and waves green claws.
Look out! He has such hungry jaws!

I wish, I wish....

Back from their class pictures, Mr. Tan's kids have constructed a huge picture frame and are filling it with written phrases that tell their fears and feelings and jokes about having their pictures taken...

Oh! My teeth are crooked. My hair is awful. My nose is disgusting. Why did I wear this green sweater? I wish I was in the back row.

The multi-grade middle school class has collected over 100 Figures of Speech on their Graffiti Mural. Now they are writing stories ... or poems ... or essays ... or articles ... or dialogues ... all using 20 or more Figures of Speech. Here's one...

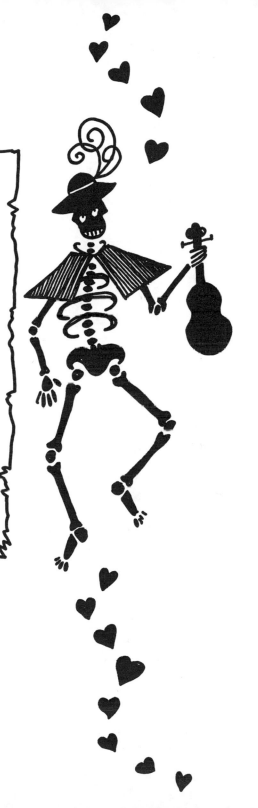

IS THERE A SKELETON IN YOUR CLOSET?

Everyone thinks I'm the big cheese in math class. But the real truth is that I have to beat my brains out on every assignment. Today the cat got out of the bag. Everyone saw right through me.

It was a lousy day anyway. I was down in the dumps the minute I woke up. Studying last night wasn't worth a hill of beans and I knew I'd be in a pretty pickle when I got to math class. My brother was getting in my hair and driving me up a wall. Mom was fit to be tied when he and I got in a big fight. She almost bit our heads off.

On my way to school it was raining cats and dogs, so my bike slipped on a corner and I bit the dust. At school the math teacher was pretty burned up because none of us had finished our homework. I shook in my boots as he passed out the test, because I knew I was in hot water. I was especially up a creek on the algebra problems. I blew the test.

I kept a stiff upper lip at school, but I sure needed to let off some steam. I held my tongue until I got into my room where I could throw things and scream my head off. One shoe went through the window— and now I'm really in the dog house.

In the seventh grade Social Studies class, students have added to their life-sized portraits large words describing the various roles they fill in the various social groups of their lives...

STUDENT....DAUGHTER....STEP-SON....SOCCER PLAYER....FRIEND....
HORSE RIDER....NEIGHBOR....BIG BROTHER....LAWN MOWER....
BABYSITTER....TUTOR....WRITER....PET OWNER....GROUCH....

Now they are writing role autobiographies describing the norms of behavior for one or more of the roles.

Romancing kids into writing has two components. First, there is the **motivation.** You've seen examples of those on the past few pages. Second, there is what I call **Collecting Impressions.** It is an excited—sometimes noisy and even frenzied—gathering of thoughts, feelings, phrases, memories that starts with one budding idea and blooms into gardens of related impressions. One possibility romances—and others grow and spread from it with the fever of a blossoming love affair.

It is this two-part romance that supplied the raw material for the writing going on in the classrooms we've just visited. The process works the same way for all of the writers I know. My songwriter friend Don has a briefcase littered with scraps of paper containing scribbled lines and parts of verses that eventually become lyrics. Carol, my poet-neighbor, has stacks of cards with snipits she's collecting for her new book. And the stacks of files and computer disks my husband has filled with thoughts, quotes, and possible writing material have literally taken over every surface of his office.

Isn't this what writing is? ... the combining of notions and parts of ideas into final, precise (well, sometimes precise) works? How can children truly have the experience of writing, then, unless they have been given the time and incitement to gather the ideas?

I have this notion that ideas are sequestered some place inside us—maybe in heads or hearts or limbs or stomachs—and that a teacher's task is to offer keys and jolts and maps so the ideas can be unlocked or jarred loose and travel out through mouths and pencils and fingertips at keyboards.

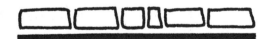

BIAS #12
IT'S HARD TO WRITE IN A VACUUM

Writing ISN'T taught by saying, "Write...," and then scoring what kids already know how to do. It IS taught by offering challenging directions, presenting patterns, and providing endless examples that open doors to original expression.

Even adults (including those who make their living as writers) need catalysts—not every time they pick up a pencil or sit in front of a computer, but as a continuing force in their creative lives. So don't be afraid to provide a theme or offer a form or plant an idea. (But DO be open enough to allow the writing to go in any direction or flexible enough to permit total deviation from your idea.)

Giving a writing assignment **could** consist of saying...

Write an advertisement for this jar of peanut butter.

This is NOT what I mean by *offering direction.* I mean...get to work romancing the student with this idea so thoroughly that she is intimate with that jar of peanut butter...

she knows how it smells and tastes
she knows how it spreads on fresh bread
she's licked it from her fingers
she's had it stuck to the roof of her mouth
she's found out how other people like it
she's familiar with its ingredients
she's read and heard and watched other ads for products
she has a collection of descriptive words and related feelings
she has a collection of convincing slogans for selling it...

... even before she begins to write that ad.

This is ROMANCE—by the time the writer begins the writing, she is already loaded with raw material. The writing is not this struggle to *think of something.* Many *somethings* are already on hand, jotted down in lists, notes, charts, webs, or whatever. Romance takes much of the hesitation, the pain, and the panic out of writing! And romance replaces these with something else. Instead of hesitation—eagerness. Instead of pain—comfort. Instead of panic— confidence.

Instead of, *I can't think of anything—*

it's, *Yes, I have something to say!*

ROMANCING WRITERS WITH LITERATURE

Literature is the best stimulator for writing that I know. Make it a point to **saturate** your students with literature—all kinds—all the time. There are literally hundreds of ways to use the written word to inspire young writers to pick up pens and make their own literature.

START WITH A WHOLE BOOK...

Anybody of any age (yes, your high school kids, too) can relate to *Alexander and the Terrible, Horrible, No-Good, Very Bad Day* by Judith Viorst, because **everybody** has some terrible, horrible days in life! Enjoy the book with your students... then share orally your *bad day* experiences. Enjoy laughing and groaning together about them. Collect lists of stuff that makes for a bad day. Then write...

... the 10 things that happened to you on your very worst day.

... OR the story of the most horrible day of your life.

... OR the story of a horrible day that didn't happen, and you surely hope it never does.

... OR a directory of things to say (or not to say) to a person who is having an awful day.

... OR 10 things that might happen to make a very GOOD day.

OR...START WITH PART OF A BOOK...

Many books (and not just fiction) have captivating beginnings and stopping places just right for enticing writers to carry on the tale. *Fortunately* by Remy Charlip is one—a good news-bad news story:

Fortunately one day, Ned got a letter that said,
"Please come to a surprise party."
Unfortunately, the party was in Florida and he was in New York.
Fortunately, a friend loaned him an airplane.
Unfortunately, the motor exploded.
Fortunately, there was a parachute in the airplane.

Groups or individuals can finish the story by adding at least 3 more *fortunately* and 3 more *unfortunately* statements orally or in writing.

OR ... USE SOME BRIEF SELECTIONS FROM A BOOK... . ♥ . ♥ . ♥ . ♥ . ♥ . ♥

Read some cures from Alvin Schwartz's wonderful book of American folklore *Cross Your Fingers, Spit in Your Hat,* such as...

If you catch a cold, fry some onions, mix them with turpentine, and spread them on your chest... or kiss a mule.

If freckles cause you to suffer... rub on ripe strawberries or cucumber slices or cover them for a few minutes each day with mud or cow manure.

If you catch the chicken pox, lie on the floor of a chicken house and get somebody to chase a flock of hens over you.

Hold a lively discussion on possible ailments that folks might want cured and imagine some remedies or cures. Then write your own *prescriptions* for curing hiccups or moles or sore throats or mumps or curly hair or no hair or broken bones or the flu or warts or sniffles or measles or a bad memory or a headache or acne or a broken heart.

. ♥ . ♥ . ♥ . ♥ . ♥ . ♥ OR ... SHARE A POEM TO IMITATE... . ♥ . ♥ . ♥ . ♥

Start with a poem of interest to kids. Then talk about the idea, the form, the poet's approach. Try to mimic either the style, the form, or the theme of the poem and create your own. The poem **"This Is Just To Say"** by William Carols Williams is a wonderful one to imitate. It presents a universal theme, one that kids love.

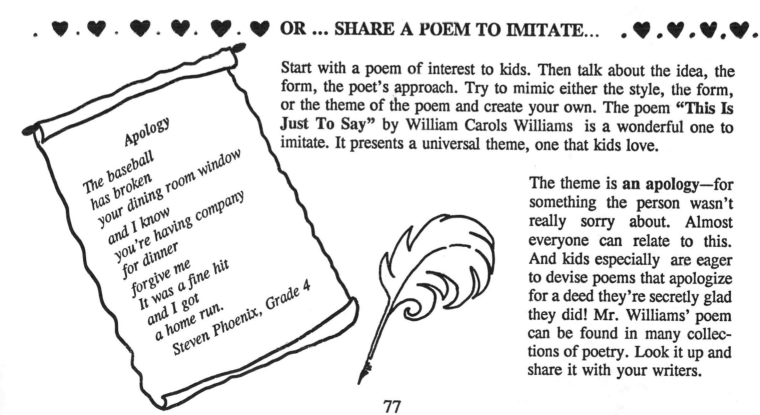

Apology

The baseball
has broken
your dining room window
and I know
you're having company
for dinner
forgive me
It was a fine hit
and I got
a home run.
Steven Phoenix, Grade 4

The theme is **an apology**—for something the person wasn't really sorry about. Almost everyone can relate to this. And kids especially are eager to devise poems that apologize for a deed they're secretly glad they did! Mr. Williams' poem can be found in many collections of poetry. Look it up and share it with your writers.

77

OR ... LOOK CLOSELY AT ONE KIND OF LITERATURE...

For instance, delve into news articles. Get to know the style of writing, the topics of interest, the kinds of words and phrases and techniques reporters use to grab readers' interest. Then take a familiar story or incident, and put it into *news language.*

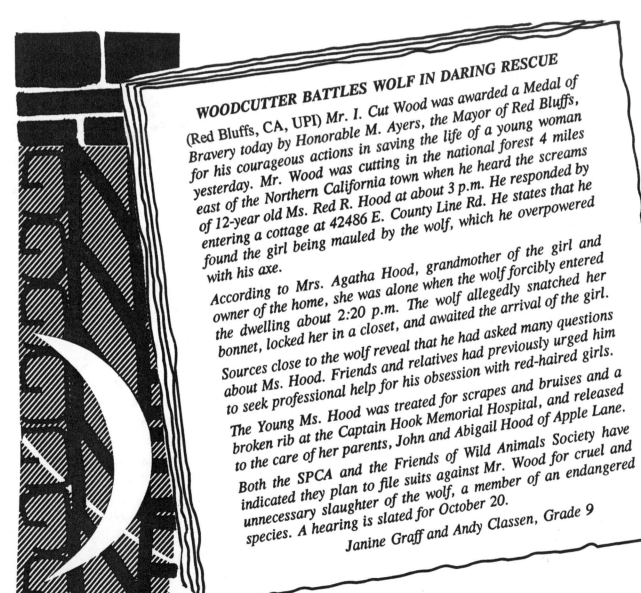

WOODCUTTER BATTLES WOLF IN DARING RESCUE

(Red Bluffs, CA, UPI) Mr. I. Cut Wood was awarded a Medal of Bravery today by Honorable M. Ayers, the Mayor of Red Bluffs, for his courageous actions in saving the life of a young woman yesterday. Mr. Wood was cutting in the national forest 4 miles east of the Northern California town when he heard the screams of 12-year old Ms. Red R. Hood at about 3 p.m. He responded by entering a cottage at 42486 E. County Line Rd. He states that he found the girl being mauled by the wolf, which he overpowered with his axe.

According to Mrs. Agatha Hood, grandmother of the girl and owner of the home, she was alone when the wolf forcibly entered the dwelling about 2:20 p.m. The wolf allegedly snatched her bonnet, locked her in a closet, and awaited the arrival of the girl.

Sources close to the wolf reveal that he had asked many questions about Ms. Hood. Friends and relatives had previously urged him to seek professional help for his obsession with red-haired girls.

The Young Ms. Hood was treated for scrapes and bruises and a broken rib at the Captain Hook Memorial Hospital, and released to the care of her parents, John and Abigail Hood of Apple Lane. Both the SPCA and the Friends of Wild Animals Society have indicated they plan to file suits against Mr. Wood for cruel and unnecessary slaughter of the wolf, a member of an endangered species. A hearing is slated for October 20.

Janine Graff and Andy Classen, Grade 9

OR ... SHARE A PIECE ON A PARTICULAR THEME...

Listen to the poem *Love Song for a Jellyfish* by Sandra Hochman. Then write your own odes, tributes, or love songs to unusual things or objects ... your old sneakers, your nose, a porcupine, lightning bugs, pizza, thunderstorms, fog, a shark, December, romance, your past, high school, a math test, your soccer ball...

* * * * * * *

To September

I've dreaded your arrival
Looked forward to you, too
Oh, month of new beginnings,
I'm glad, yet scared of you

New classes, new teachers,
New chances, new shoes
Old worries, old habits,
Old friends with new news

You bring each one back
I'm nervous you're here
And excited, September
You start the school year.

Tom & Chad, Grade 10

Love Song To My Eraser

Oh, eraser on my pencil's end
How long you've been my teeth-marked friend!
How many times have you been bit?
I love you so, I cannot quit!
My teeth chomped in one time too many,
Oh, no, my pencil top is empty!   ....Vicki, Grade 8

Song To My Teddy Bear

Teddy bear, I like your fuzzy fur.
I like the way you hug me.
You never yell at me or act bossy or hurt my feelings.
You're always around when I need you.
Oh, teddy bear, I'll keep you forever.

Dictated by Brie, Grade 1

To My Chicken Pox

To chicken pox
Your polka dots
Have left me
Full of fancy spots.

I have 10 thousand
Well, maybe not quite
But I'm red and white
And I itch all night.

Go to Mars
And don't leave scars
Goodbye spots, itchy socks
Get lost, chicken pox!

Shana, Grade 5

* * * * * * * * * * * * * *

OR ... USE A CYCLE OF PIECES ON ONE THEME...

Listen to a "cycle" of pieces of literature on one theme. Try to find several different kinds of pieces on the same theme or topic. For example, bring a news article, a joke, an essay, a poem, an advertisement, and a description all related to the same topic. Then students can add to the cycle by writing another piece on the same theme.

Everyone knows about *WARNINGS*. We've been warned all our lives about things to do or not to do. Look for *warnings* in literature, such as: ***Early Bird*** and ***Warning*** by Shel Silverstein, ***If You Should Meet a Crocodile*** (author unknown), Odgen Nash's ***The Panther***, David McCord's ***Glowworm***, and ***Don't Ever Seize a Weasel by the Tail*** by Jack Prelutsky. Make lists of things that you've been warned about (and consequences of doing them). Use these ideas to write your own warnings. (Add illustrations to make **Warning Posters!**)

If you cross your eyes,
They'll probably stick.
If you eat with dirt
* under your fingernails*
You'll end up sick.
*   Jane, Grade 1*

Never tickle an elephant,
For when an elephant begins to
Grin
Cackle
Laugh
And giggle,
An elephant loses her balance
And begins to topple
And you never want to be close
To a falling elephant!
*   Sharon, Grade 3*

Listen to your mother
And eat your vegetables
And don't pick on your brother
And never drink coffee
And always wear clean underwear
And turn out the light
If you don't... what will happen?
Well... something just might!
*   Maria Elena, Grade 4*

Watch out! Take care!
Watch out who you trust.
Just because someone is clever,
Or speaks well,
Or is well-educated,
Or is an adult,
Doesn't mean they are right.
*   Kai, Grade 11*

OR ... FOCUS ON A FAMILIAR OR FAVORITE FORM...

Take a second look at some of those favorite forms of literature...
maybe even the short or simple ones kids loved as young children,
such as nursery rhymes, fairy tales, couplets, jumprope rhymes,
fables, proverbs, couplets. Pay close attention to the way the form is
written and the kinds of ideas that are included. Have kids try to
mimic, re-write, revise, or otherwise add their own touch to the form
as they work toward some original renditions!

A group of kids of all ages listened to and talked about many old
proverbs such as...

A rolling stone gathers no moss.
Fools rush in where angels fear to tread.
A bird in the hand is worth two in the bush.
A stitch in time saves nine.
A penny saved is a penny earned.
Strike while the iron is hot.
Fish and visitors smell in three days.
Don't change horses in the middle of the stream.
Don't count your chickens before they hatch.
You can lead a horse to water but you can't make it drink.

And then they wrote their own...

A rolling stone gathers no <u>rhythm</u>.
Fools rush in where <u>there's lots of money</u>.
<u>Garbage</u> and <u>socks</u> smell in three days.
A penny saved is <u>your start on a fortune</u>.
A bird in the hand is worth <u>a pie in the face</u>.
A penny saved is <u>not much</u>.
<u>Don't fool around</u> while the iron is hot.
You can lead a horse to water, but you <u>can't drink the water</u>.
Fools rush in where <u>there is food</u>.
A bird in the hand is worth <u>a bird in the hand</u>.
Don't count your chickens <u>before you feed them</u>.
<u>Iron</u> while the iron is hot.
Don't change <u>your pants</u> in the middle of the stream.

ROMANCING WRITERS WITH MUSIC

LISTEN TO WORDLESS MUSIC...

..and let the melodies and moods and rhythms inspire...

word lists
lines and phrases
song lyrics
descriptions of feelings
word-images
letters
thoughts or feelings
dramas or dialogues
slogans or protests
poems or chants
an imagined description of the music's creator

Try music of differing styles, moods, rhythms, types, backgrounds, and time periods, adapting the writing suggestions to match the piece.

OR ... LISTEN TO MUSIC WITH WORDS...

..and then, after you listen...

... change the words
... add a verse
... invent titles
... design record covers
... write some different lyrics on the same theme

For instance: after you listen to *A Friend Like Me,* the popular tune from Disney's *Aladdin* movie, write...

... a word portrait of what you'd like to have in a friend
... a tribute to your friend
... a list of 10 friendly things to do
... disadvantages of having a genie for a friend
... an adventure shared by a group of friends
... a tale about an unusual friend

ROMANCING WRITERS WITH ART

The visual arts stimulate *painting with words* and, likewise, writing leads easily to creating with color and form. Since the two flow so naturally together, try mixing them often in your classroom.

Have kids create brilliant banners and flags of many colors using food coloring, paint & sponges, or watercolor washes. OR... they might fill paper with colored-chalk designs that emphasize ONE color. This yields wonderful visual pieces **and** much excitement about color! Next, they'll be ready to start associating particular colors with tastes, sounds, smells, sights, thoughts, feelings, places, and experiences that contribute raw material for written pieces such as...

Really Red

Sirens screaming
Stoplights flashing
Babies crying
Spaghetti cooking
These are red.
Cinnamon red stings your tongue
And bites your nose with cold wind
Red is angry words
And embarrassment
Disneyland is red
        Georgia, Grade 5

Blue

Blue is the smell of a pie baking
And the taste of jam.
Going down a waterslide is blue.
My fingers get blue in the winter.
Blue is when your best friend moves
Or you get left out of a game.
Blue is oceans, bruises and smoke.
Blue is sleeping on a new pillow.
        Elijah, Grade 2

Pickles & Stomach Aches

Green is broccoli and snakes,
Pickles and the park in spring.
Christmas is green.
The sound of a croaking frog,
The taste of moldy cottage cheese,
The smell of newly-mown grass.
Green is music,
Green is the feeling you have when
you've eaten a whole pizza.
        Thomas, Grade 4

Independent Yellow

Yellow never wants help
but steps right out on its own
throwing bright light everywhere.
It dashes through flower gardens
Splashes on fried eggs
Drips on traffic lights
And wraps itself around bananas.
Yellow reaches out from the sun
And never gives up.
Yellow is BOLD.
        DeAnne & Michael, Grade 11

83

ROMANCING WRITERS WITH THEMSELVES

Everybody has a ME. Everyone knows some things about her or his SELF. So the topic is an immediate motivator for all ages.

Gather up some pocket mirrors, and ask kids to bring old snapshots of themselves from home (showing how they *used to look*). Once everyone has a mirror and a picture, start comparing today's selves to younger selves. Ask kids to think about their then-and-now physical appearance, favorite things to do, hobbies, beliefs, fears, likes and dislikes, friends, etc. Then ask them to try writing in a form which repeats lines such as this...

I Used To Be

I used to be chubby
But now I'm thin.

I used to be messy
But now I'm neat.

I used to hate boys
But now I only hate them a little.

I used to be clumsy
But now I'm coordinated.

I used to be afraid of big kids
But now I'm a big kid.

I used to be nine
But now I'm ten.

> *Janice, Grade 5*

Then and Now

I used to be a little runt,
But now I'm kind of tough.

I used to have a few freckles,
But now I have thousands.

I used to hate math,
But now I can do Algebra.

I used to be terrified of thunder,
But now it's earthquakes I fear.

I used to want a skateboard
really bad,
But now I want a snowboard
really bad.

> *Erik, Grade 7*

ME

I used to have short curls, but now I have long, straight hair.
I used to be best friends with Amy, but now she's moved away.
I used to have dad read me stories, but now I read them myself.
I used to be into fingerpainting, but now I'm into the trampoline.
I used to be in kindergarten, but now I'm in second grade.
> *Yolanda, Grade 2*

There are more ME ideas in Chapter 11.

ROMANCING WRITERS WITH MOVEMENT

Moving the body awakens creative thinking and rouses the words that help express ideas and interpret feelings.

Try moving like various animals or natural forces or mechanical inventions. At the same time, write phrases that express **movement**...

a swirling, howling wind
flounder and flail like a fish on dry land
oozing, melting butter
a lumbering, clumsy elephant
deafening, screeching jackhammer
water gushing and leaping over a waterfall
tearing around sharp corners like a roller coaster
a slouching, slinking panther
meandering along like a lazy river
chipmunks all a-scurry
monotonous up & down, up & down rhythm of a pump

And ... if you're going to **write** about a lion, first spend some time...

MOVING like a lion ... sleeping in the tall grass
     ... waking and yawning
     ... stalking its prey
     ... prowling through grasslands
     ... playing with cubs
     ... defending its territory
     ... protecting its cubs
     ... devouring dinner
     ... caged in a zoo

THEN write   *... some LION-sized words*
     ... lion sounds
     ... lion tales
     ... lion names
     ... lion movements
     ... lion lies
     ... lion adventures
     ... lion conversations

Some of the best writing *happenings* arise spontaneously out of a need to release a feeling that's rampant in the classroom. It may be…

> … *excitement over an accomplishment.*
> … *anticipation of a special occasion.*
> … *anxiety about an upcoming challenge.*
> … *disappointment over a change in plans.*
> … *anger resulting from a specific event.*
> … *jealousy at missing out on something.*

Talking and writing about those feelings often helps them to be savored, understood, defused, or re-directed.

Once my class returned from music with hostility running high over alleged insults to one student from their music teacher. They wanted to rant and rave and go on attacking this teacher. I encouraged them to start *what really makes me mad* statements and gradually led complaints away from the individual to general irritating situations in their world. Soon we were laughing together instead of grumbling!

Then, I asked students to work alone or in pairs to make personal *Don't You Just It Hate When…* lists. I made my own. We had a wonderful time sharing them and a good experience sharing legitimate anger in an appropriate, non-destructive manner.

Here's one such list started by a teacher. You can probably add some of your own…

Don't you just hate it when…*you get a new student—and nobody bothered to tell you ahead of time?*

Don't you just hate it when…*the principal comes to observe you just at the moment that one kid is biting another?*

Don't you just hate it when…*the fire bell rings just after everyone has settled down and finally started to work?*

ROMANCING WRITERS WITH ... JUST TALKING

You know how great those times are when someone starts to tell a personal anecdote, and immediately others start to chime in with, *"Oh, yeah!—I've had that happen too!"* Some very rewarding writing experiences emerge from shared memories, common feelings, and familiar happenings. Sometimes YOU can start this process. Other times it just happens ... and you need to be ready to grab hold of it.

One day, I got carried away recounting to a group of kids some not-so-memorable memories from my past—such as...

> ... *the time I had to stand in the wastebasket for a whole period in 8th grade Social Studies for talking during a test.*

> ... *the spanking I got for giving a little perfume bottle full of water from the toilet to my least favorite aunt.*

> ... *the day I gave a speech to 200 people—with my zipper open.*

After sharing memories and happenings, the kids wanted to write...

> ... *the most embarrassing situation of my life.*
> ... *the worst trouble I've ever been in.*
> ... *the stupidest thing I did when I was little.*
> ... *the stupidest thing I've done recently.*
> ... *something that happened to me in kindergarten.*
> ... *something I'm really glad happened to me.*
> ... *my first day of high school or...violin lesson...or bike ride...or kiss ...or soccer practice...or spanking...or recital...or valentine...*

ROMANCING WRITERS WITH ADVENTURES

A thunderstorm that passes your window ... a wasp that sneaks into your classroom ... a walk around the block ... a popcorn party ... a game you lost in gym class ... the football team about to play for a championship. .. a fire drill that just interrupted the math test ... a class trip ... a mouse you brought in to visit the group ... yearbook pictures being taken today ... all are provokers of thoughts and feelings, words and ideas that provide the raw materials for writing.

Unpack a grocery bag filled with fruits and vegetables (some of them unusual, such as a mango, rutabaga, a jicama, or a pomegranate). Do lots of tasting and talking. This can result in word lists, riddles, descriptive paragraphs, advertisements, essays, poems and other written responses such as these done by a multi-aged group of kids...

I'm like an onion, covered with just as many layers. As you peel off each layer you get closer to who I really am. Like the onion whose strong smell may keep tasters away, I give off a message that says, "Leave me alone." But if you go to the trouble to keep peeling the layers, you'll find my distinct taste, like that of the onion, will add flavor to your life.

Toni, Grade 12

Who Am I?

I'm sumptuous
And tender and juicy—
Delicious with cream or alone.
My skin is soft as velvet
But my heart is hard as stone.

10 Reasons to Ban Watermelon

1. *It's sloppy.*
2. *It's noisy to eat.*
3. *It messes up the refrigerator.*
4. *It mushes up the fruit salad.*
5. *It stains your clothes.*
6. *The seeds are tempting to spit.*
7. *It crowds the garbage.*
8. *It breaks the grocery bag.*
9. *You have to buy more than you want.*
10. *You always have to throw out a lot and the children in Africa are starving.* ***It's The Pits!***

James, Jenny, Tom, Grade 7

Don't ever feed me hot peppers because...
The taste I couldn't stand
I'd rather swallow goldfish live
Or chew an entire rock band.

Sarah, Grade 3

ROMANCING WRITERS WITH CONTENT AREA EXPERIENCES

Watch for those times when imagination and writing skills can grow out of a lesson, unit, or activity in other curriculum areas.

One fourth grade science class, studying a unit on weather, concluded each experiment by concocting a news article—complete with a smashing headline—to summarize and show off the results of the experiment. When they put their newspapers together, they enjoyed reading and sharing both serious and frivolous science news reports.

WHICH ROMANCERS ARE RIGHT FOR YOUR WRITERS?

Here is some advice for you to consider as you choose ways to romance writers from this book or other sources:

- **Include a variety of experiences during the year.** Not all writers prefer the same selections or have the same interests or get sparked by the same assignments. Gather enough options to appeal to every kid. Your chances for reaching every writer will be much greater if you try many directions. In addition, you'll be providing a well-rounded balance of writing topics, genres, and styles.

- **Listen to your students.** Watch what they like, what they relate to, what they CAN do. Listen to them in the lunchroom, in the halls, in the washrooms, on the playground. Pay attention to their schemes and wishes and dreams and opinions and complaints. Use the stuff that's IN them... and draw upon the things they KNOW.

- **Don't overdose on romancers.** It isn't necessary to start with a hot new experience every time you write. Every group of kids needs chances to JUST write. If you're filling kids up with literature and other experiences regularly, that input accumulates. Those stimuli hang around and contribute to future writing.

- **Expand kids' horizons.** Kids love new things and new ideas. And they **need** to be exposed to happenings and facts and ideas that they've never heard. This is learning! So don't focus **only** on their current interests. Find literature or other romancers that expose kids to interesting new concepts, topics, information, forms, styles, and genres of writing.

- **Listen to yourself.** YOU are an individual too. Not all teachers prefer the same approaches or activities; different things work for different people. You might bring out a bowl of fruit as a writing motivator and find your kids spitting watermelon seeds across the room at each other. Then you'll wonder... *What on earth was Marge Frank thinking when she wrote THIS dumb idea?* What works for me may not work for you, so start with the ideas that excite you, first. Then gradually experiment with new ones. If one is a flop, don't feel like a rotten teacher. There are hundreds of other ways!

- **Don't let your lessons hold back individuals.**
  There will be many times when a student doesn't click with the lesson or doesn't need the input that day. Getting stirred up to write is needed. But for some kids, at some times, it happens so fast that they're way ahead of you. Or they're stirred up and ready before you even start. If some kids are ready to write and bursting with ideas... let them go! Everyone doesn't have to be right WITH YOU every step of the way.

- **Don't turn every great experience into a writing lesson.**
  Your students will surely rebel if every time you see a film, have a discussion, go on a trip, eat a snack, or create an artwork you turn it into a writing activity. This will surely dampen enthusiasm for those adventures. Plus ... they'll grow to hate writing.

HERE I AM ... IN THE MIDDLE OF THE PROCESS...

Right! WRITING is work! The past several months attest to that for me. Many times this summer, I have wished that you and your students could be watching over my shoulder—because what I'm trying to tell you about the writing process is what I'm doing right now!

I came to this project with plenty of writing-related experiences. My family filled my early years with literary appreciation and love of words, and I've given long hours to written assignments as a high school student, college English major, and graduate student. Recently I spent months in a virtual non-stop preparation for a series of writing seminars with teachers. I've read everything I could find on the subject. I've taken copious notes, pawed through children's books and poetry anthologies and stacks of kids' writing I've saved. I've even gone back and read my own childhood writings (which my mother was wise enough to save). I've sorted through my beliefs, visited classrooms to write with kids of all ages, presented countless workshops, and talked with hundreds of teachers all over the country. AND ... I've written other books ... and articles ... and speeches. So this book ought to be an easy job—wouldn't you think?

AND YET, in spite of my writing experience—and in spite of my many bulging file boxes labeled "stuff for Writing Book"—I've still traipsed home from bookstores loaded with new books and I've holed up for days in libraries reading articles. I've added folders full of new impressions to my files, tried out scores of thoughts on teacher-friends, and worn ragged the pages of my word-finder and thesaurus. The basic outline has been reworked nine times. Every time I've met with the artist, I've come home to make a load of changes. I've written and re-written, thrown away and started over, rearranged chapters, deleted and added and adapted.

There is struggle and sweat and resistance and restlessness. Sometimes every phrase is agony. But there is also joy and pleasure and excitement. When everything is RIGHT—and sentences are flowing spontaneously—the exhilaration can hardly be contained. Sometimes the writing is coming so fast that my fingers at the keys can hardly keep up with the words.

Students should be told about the energy it takes to write. We need to share with them the WHOLE picture—the WHOLE process—through all the romantic and unromantic phases. We must be honest about the time, the work, the joy, the pain, the fulfillment, the reluctance. Let's not ever deceive them into thinking that anybody is consistently able to sit down and command beautifully-stated, carefully-organized thoughts and ideas to drip off the end of a pencil!

92

4

The PROCESS

Writing IS A Process
The Writing Process ... A 10-Stage Plan
Ifs ... Ands ... and Buts...
What The Teacher Does While The Kids Write
"But That All Takes So Much Time," You're Saying!
A Sample Lesson Through All 10 Stages

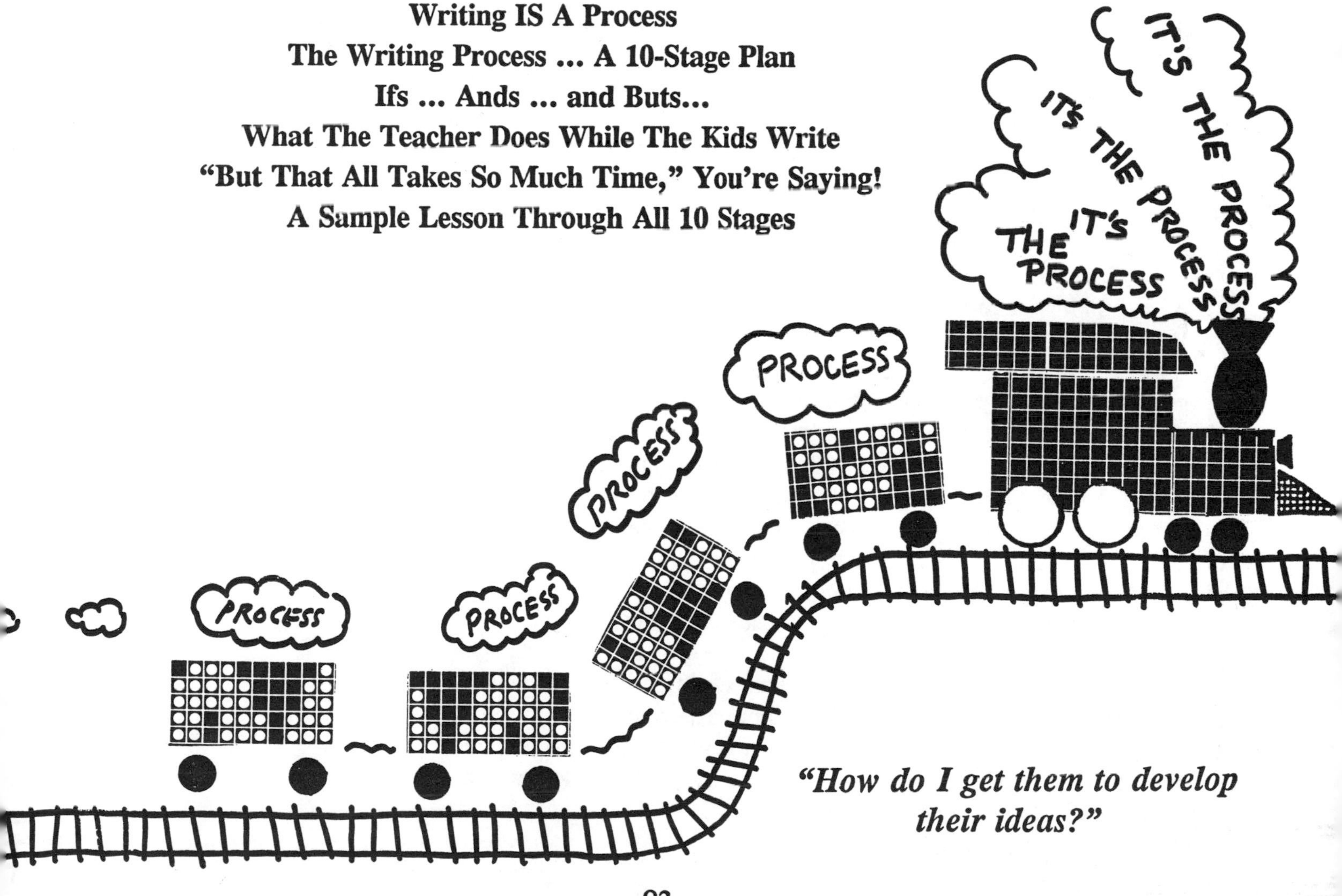

IT'S THE PROCESS
IT'S THE PROCESS
IT'S THE PROCESS

PROCESS

PROCESS

PROCESS

PROCESS

"How do I get them to develop their ideas?"

WRITING IS A PROCESS

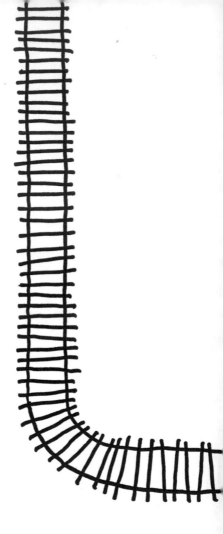

The great, inspiring ideas are not enough.
Creating technically correct sentences isn't enough either.
Writing is a whole lot more.

Writing is a thinking and doing process, a process with many phases—all of them related and intertwined. It is one of those processes that is a vital tool for life. If students are to use this tool with dexterity, they need to learn an approach to the whole process that can be applied over and over again whenever they write.

That's why this chapter presents a plan for helping students learn and use **the whole writing process**—a plan that, once learned, is forever theirs. The ten stages of the writing process that follow comprise an approach for guiding students **from beginning blunderings through to polished pieces.** This particular plan is built upon my observations of the way writing happens for teachers and kids of all ages.

There is nothing sacred about the number ten. Others may describe the writing process in three, four, or six stages. I arrived at these steps as I tried to take the process apart and explain how writers seem to proceed in moving from an initial idea through to a finished piece. If you watch a writer at work, you may find it hard to identify or count specific stages, so the exact number hardly matters. Often the parts of the process all melt and blend together to become a natural flow, and there is little separation between parts or stages. I've taken the process apart here because it is just easier to explain in smaller pieces. Furthermore, when teaching writing, it is helpful for both teacher and for writers if each stage is made conscious.

There is also no rule that says writers proceed in an orderly fashion through all ten stages. Not every writing experience gets to the *polished* and *published* stages. Even when a writer does go after a precise finished product, she may get there by going back through any number of stages any number of times.

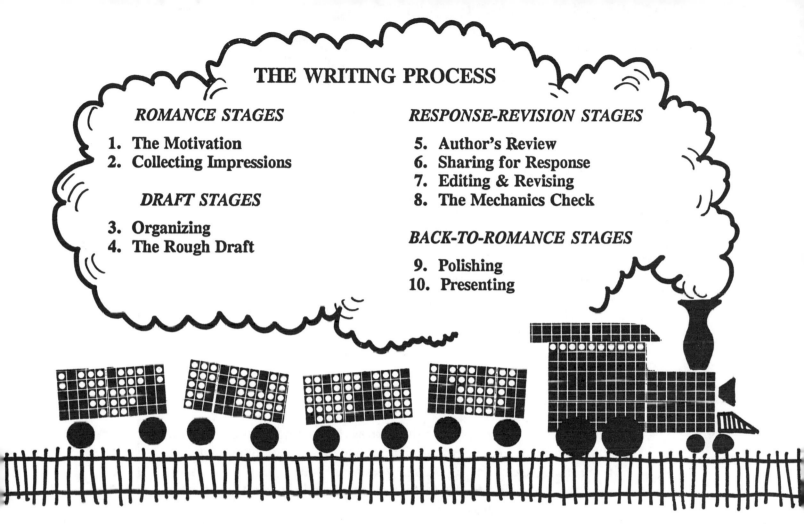

THE WRITING PROCESS

ROMANCE STAGES

1. The Motivation
2. Collecting Impressions

DRAFT STAGES

3. Organizing
4. The Rough Draft

RESPONSE-REVISION STAGES

5. Author's Review
6. Sharing for Response
7. Editing & Revising
8. The Mechanics Check

BACK-TO-ROMANCE STAGES

9. Polishing
10. Presenting

This chapter describes the writing process in general from the first romantic, exciting motivation and idea-gathering part through the hard work of drafting, reviewing, and revising, to the final (again romantic) rewards of sharing or showing off a polished piece. Other chapters (2,3,5,6,7,10) will present the why and the how-to of the individual stages and address some of the questions and problems that arise in the midst of them.

Before you try the plan, please take note of the IFs, ANDs and BUTs ... which follow it (pages 104-107). These are some cautions, recommendations, and elaborations about the use of the plan that are **just as important** to its workings as are the ten steps.

THE WRITING PROCESS
A 10-Stage Plan That Works

THE ROMANCE STAGES

STAGE 1   THE MOTIVATION

- ... a group experience
- ... an individual experience
- ... a piece of literature
- ... an unexpected happening
- ... a common feeling
- ... a question
- ... a memory
- ... a discussion
- ... a surprise happening
- ... an activity in any content area

The motivation is something that sparks the writing. You provide the situation or make use of a natural one to evoke ideas, fancies, impressions, emotions, opinions, questions, beliefs, explorations, or mysteries—to bring to the surface those possibilities and imaginings which are tucked away in minds.

Notes:

- *Suggest a direction but be loose enough to allow others.*

- *Engage kids with loads of **different** kinds of motivators.*

- *Choose high-interest motivators—the ones that fascinate kids and the ones that are important for life.*

- *See Chapters 2, 3, and 11 for dozens of ways to romance kids into writing and/or stimulate specific writing experiences.*

- *Don't miss out on the natural motivators that linger all the time in classrooms. They're usually better than any you could concoct!*

STAGE 2   COLLECTING IMPRESSIONS

... the gathering of words and fragments and thoughts and facts and phrases and questions and observations ... the process of brainstorming about and broadening of the original idea...

Notes:

- *This is a fast, fun stage—even dizzying sometimes. Let it happen naturally and flow along quickly, with students contributing spontaneously all kinds of possibilities related to the topic. The idea is to gather as much raw material as possible, and to keep collecting until you get past the ordinary stuff to the new, fresh, and unusual.*

- *Most of us need this stage the most. It is **crucial** to the growth of creative thinking. And it is a critical step for generating the content of the writing. Way too often teachers and writers do too little of this. We're so anxious to move on to finished products that we quit collecting too soon. **Don't cut this short!** Allow plenty of time for this stage in your writing sessions.*

- *Keep individual (or class) notebooks with collections of words, phrases, sentences, impressions, and ideas. Students can use later what they don't use in today's writing.*

- *When you collect impressions with kids, take **everything** they suggest. Encourage writers to do this when they work alone—to write down everything that comes to mind. It's far better to have too many ideas than too few. Writers can always sort, censor, choose, replace, or eliminate later.*

- *YOU contribute your impressions too. Don't take over the process, but realize that your additions will encourage divergence in thinking, teach new words, show kids how to elaborate on existing ideas, and share yourself.*

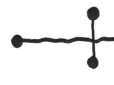
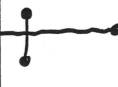

THE DRAFT STAGES

STAGE 3   ORGANIZING

... the time for taking a close look at all those impressions you have collected and thinking about what fits together...

This is the time for asking yourself questions such as...

What goes with this idea?
Which ideas should be grouped together?
Where would this fit into the whole picture?
What do these ideas or phrases have in common?

... and then using some method to visually connect impressions together. Your organizational tool may be a chart, or a web, or a storyboard, or an outline, or a series of boxes, or a diagram, or a list, or series of note cards. It can be anything that groups your usable ideas together in a way that will help you go on to connecting them in your writing.

Notes:

- *There are many, many ways to do this. Indeed, there is certainly no one **right** or **best** way. The effective approaches to organizing will differ according to age and ability of writers, individual styles and needs, genre of the writing, length of time you have to think and write, and other factors. Let your writers experiment with organizational methods. Complex organization is not always better. Start simple, and stay simple, unless the form of the piece (such as essays, position papers, etc.) demand a more elaborate organizational plan.*

- ***Don't overdo this.*** *I've seen kids get sick to death of webs. And I've seen others gag on too many outlines. Yes, kids need to learn how to organize their ideas in preparation for writing. No, kids do not need to do an intricate organizational pattern for every piece of writing. Sometimes the writing flows along well from collecting right into the draft—and stopping to organize interferes with the inspiration that's carrying the writer along.*

STAGE 4   THE ROUGH DRAFT

... the put-it-together phase...

This is the stage at which you say, *"Okay, you've got thoughts and groups of ideas and phrases. You've thought about which of these may fit together. Now ... write!"* Start putting those words together into phrases, those phrases together into lines or sentences, those sentences together into paragraphs.

Notes:

- *Do you remember the last time YOU faced a blank page? Maybe you had to write a reference for a colleague, or a thank you note for a gift you couldn't stand, or your professional goals for a graduate school application. PANIC ... right? Remember this pain when you ask kids to write. Then help ease the rough-draft panic by...*

  ... letting them write without stopping to make corrections and spell words right. You can always go back and fix errors later. You can't always recover a lost train of thought.

  ... struggling through it together as a group—many times. This will give students practice and patterns for doing it alone.

  ... allowing and encouraging sharing as they work. The open communication that arises in this stage generates more ideas. The humming, somewhat noisy climate has a momentum all its own that often sweeps along even the most reluctant writers—and that isn't as likely to happen in total silence. In fact, total silence is sometimes pretty disturbing.

- *The better a job you do on stages 1,2, and 3, the less painful will be the rough draft, because you'll have so much raw material before you. This puts a big dent in the "I can't think of anything!" syndrome that often strikes draft writers.*

THE RESPONSE-REVISION STAGES

STAGE 5   AUTHOR'S REVIEW

... the author's chance to get the writing out into the light and see how it looks and hear how it sounds...

This is the time for writers to ask themselves questions such as, *"Does it make sense?" "Does it say what I intended?" "Do I like it?" "Is it smooth and clear?" "Are the ideas in the right order?" "Are any words or pieces missing?"* and other such questions that good writing teachers can help kids learn to ask.

Note:
- *This review is intended strictly for the writer. Its purpose is to get the writer used to responding to his or her own work. Reading aloud to yourself is probably the best way to do this, because your ears often catch what your eyes miss.*

STAGE 6   SHARING FOR RESPONSE

... a time for trading pieces, or reading to a small group, or sharing with the teacher—for the purpose of getting reactions, questions, suggestions, praises, affirmation of strengths, and ideas for changes...

Notes:
- *Teach students that response focuses on positive help—that it is meant to be constructive and affirming, not degrading.*

- *Kids CAN learn to do this. They NEED to learn to do this. The teacher is not by any means the only one or the best one for giving constructive feedback to writers.*

- *I ALWAYS tell kids, "YOU have the final say. You listen to others' responses and make use of those recommendations that you believe will improve your writing. You do not have to accept or make use of all the suggestions—including mine."*

STAGE 7   EDITING & REVISING

... the changing, fixing stage ... including anything from reshuffling or replacing words to reworking whole pieces...

After the writer has reviewed her own work and gained the responses of others, then she's ready to make adjustments.

Notes:

- *Confine the reworking to one or two skills or weaknesses at a time. When kids try to fix everything, efforts are so scattered that nothing is significantly improved. Revision focused on a few things is a good way to really improve the craft of writing.*

- ***Teach kids to do this**—don't do it yourself. Even very young children can learn to revise their own work.*

- *Every piece of writing does not need to get "fixed." And, definitely, each piece does not need immediate or extensive revision. Sometimes, let a piece sit a while before a writer makes changes, or excuse it from any revision at all.*

- *See Chapter 5 to help kids of all ages learn to rework writing.*

STAGE 8   THE MECHANICS CHECK

... the time to inspect the original draft for spelling, grammar, mechanical, and structural errors or weaknesses...

This may be the point at which the teacher takes papers home to note (preferably with some means other than a red pencil, please) errors in mechanics (or conventions) OR looks over shoulders to point them out. A good deal of this can also be done in student groups or with the help of peers, older students, or volunteer adults.

Note:

- *See Chapter 5 for more help on this topic and for ideas about how to get kids to do much of this by themselves.*

STAGE 9   THE FINAL COPY

... the preparation of the final draft—making use of the input of all your own and others' responses on content and techniques and mechanics ... AND the resulting satisfaction and surprise that comes with the polishing of a product...

Notes:

- *This stage brings writers back to the romance again. The hard work of organizing and drafting and reworking and examining and evaluating is done. The decisions about polishing are made. So make merry at this stage! Pay attention to the fulfillment that lurks beneath those moments of writing or dictating or keyboarding the finished piece.*

- *Don't expect that writers will always go straight from stage 1 through to stage 9. The process is fluid, and this means that there might be a lot of movement backwards as well as forwards! Stages 5-8, for instance, may be repeated one or more times before the writer chooses to begin the final copy.*

- *Don't rush towards this stage. If writers see this final copy as the real goal of the writing, the rest of the process will lose importance. Too often, young writers get the message—albeit in subtle ways—that the final copy is the only thing that matters. Yes, it is a satisfying stage. But its very existence is the result of every other stage of the process.*

- *Talk with kids about the plague that a creator of any product often suffers: that old it-could-always-be-more-perfect feeling which often accompanies the finishing of a work. Remind them that there comes a time for everyone to quit reworking and be satisfied with the product (at least for the time being).*

STAGE 10   PRESENTING

... the sharing, showing-off, or publishing part ... the chance to use your written words to communicate to other persons. In some way, every finished piece should be made public **if the author chooses...**

Note:

• *There are dozens of ways to flaunt writing. Chapter 7 suggests good reasons for sharing, along with a few dozen ideas of ordinary and not-so-ordinary ways to do it. Read these ideas and possibilities ... then add your own!*

THE WHOLE THING

On pages 112-119, you will find a sample lesson that has been broken into the ten steps of the writing process. This shows you how one teacher guided a group of students through the entire process in a group writing experience. A 4th grade class worked together to write and polish a piece of *Painted Writing* (finished piece on page 119).

IFs ... ANDs ... and BUTs ... (Cautions About The Plan)

BUT ... DON'T ALWAYS GO THROUGH ALL 10 STAGES!

If you do a complete autopsy on every piece, your writers will perish from too much pruning. They'll stop writing, or hate writing, or work really hard to make pieces very short so they don't have much work to do.

As a teacher, don't feel guilty if your class doesn't get through all 10 stages on a piece. If you stop after stage 2 or 3, **you still have had a valuable writing lesson.** Again, **each step is valuable.** Significant writing instruction happens in every phase.

In fact, **plan** lessons that only do stage 1 or stages 1-2 or 1-3 or 1-6. The more you work with parts of the process—the faster writers of all ages will learn to handle the process for themselves.

When to go through with the whole process? When not to? For some ideas about this, see the question section of Chapter 10.

BUT ... DO THEM ALL SOME OF THE TIME.

If they are never asked to refine or perfect a piece of writing, kids will quickly get the message that precision, polishing, and creating a final piece that's the result of working through the whole writing process seriously are not important. For some thoughts about when to and when not to go through the whole process, see the question-answer section of Chapter 10.

IF ... YOU THINK THE FINAL PRODUCT IS THE MOST IMPORTANT THING ... THINK AGAIN!

The process is more important than the product.
Accentuate the process. Be vocal about the fact that this is the way writers work and be honest about those unromantic stages.

Remember, **every step** of the process is just as important as the final product—actually more important, because without the others, there would be no final product. Help kids see how the final product is the result of all the other stages, and how a change in **any** of those other stages would have caused the final product to be different.

The real purpose of the plan is to help kids internalize the process. The process will become natural to them more quickly if you keep them aware of which part of the process they are doing.

Bring in real live writers (or other creators) to show students the process they go through, the many drafts and revisions. Help kids see that this is the way writing happens.

Build a bulletin board display around the stages in the writing process. This way, kids can visualize the whole process and actually *see* the value of each stage.

Share your own stuff with your students. Let them watch YOUR writing in process.

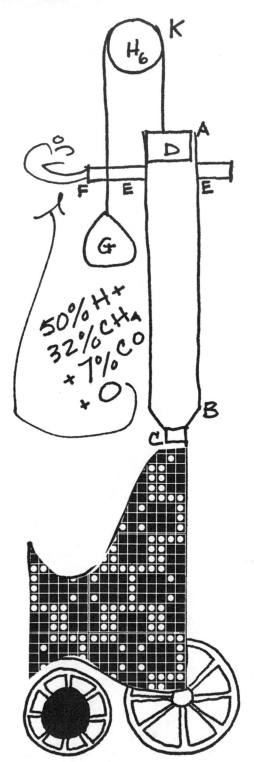

AND ... DON'T SKIP THE ROMANCE.

If kids don't want to write, or seem reluctant, or whine, *"I can't think of anything,"* or write very little while squirming with impatience and discomfort—nine times out of ten, it's because **they haven't been sufficiently romanced!**

Avoid ... at all costs ... starting with Stage 4. I have been guilty of that often enough to remember how it leaves students staring at blank pages harboring *"I CAN'T"* feelings—and to know that the cold plunge into the *"Start writing..."* stage is very likely to produce awkward, water-logged products.

Keep alert to your students' interests, and be flexible. If everyone is suddenly captivated by the crow on the window sill—stop everything to watch and write about the crow. **That is** the moment for writing— not this afternoon at two o'clock. If you adapt the writing schedule and forms to the interests of your writers, they'll be much more ready and yes, even eager, to actually pick up pencils and write.

BUT ... DON'T OVERDO THE ROMANCE EITHER.

You just can't force romance. If an assignment is dying ... bury it! Or if one kid is crazy about another idea and bursting with ideas... let him follow that. Or if a group of writers is romanced by something else, don't hold them back with a teacher-created experience.

And, **most of all ... please...** don't turn **every** exciting event or discovery or rampant feeling that occurs in your classroom into **a** writing activity. The kids may want to write about the crow the first time it shows up, but not the second and third. If kids know they have to write after every movie or every field trip—they'll surely come to dread writing. They'll hate the field trips, too.

IF ... YOU IMPROVE AT YOUR USE OF THE PROCESS... SO WILL YOUR STUDENTS.

Do it yourself. Write with your students. Focus on **your** use of the process. The better you become at handling it, the better you'll be at helping young writers.

AND ... RELAX!

So many of the teachers I know and meet get really overwhelmed trying to do a good job of teaching the writing process.

Think about this...

Every kid doesn't have to master every aspect of the writing process in **your** class **this** year. Writers have years to gain experience and expertise with the process. Sometimes we teachers think, *"If I don't teach this to these kids now, they'll never get it."*

Don't force perfecting of the whole process on your students. Don't expect them—even at high school level—to become proficient at doing a thorough job with each stage on each piece of writing after they've been in your class three, six, or even nine months. Just work away, a bit at a time, at various stages in the process and various skills that are naturally a part of each stage. Keep trying different forms of writing. Keep giving them as many interesting adventures with words and language as you can squeeze into your class time. And, if you do ... believe me, your writers will improve.

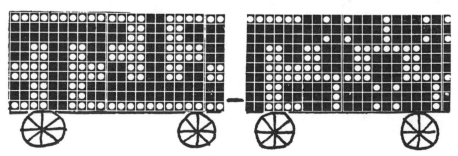

WHAT THE TEACHER DOES WHILE THE KIDS WRITE

A classroom full of writers looks like this ... people are writing, thinking, mumbling, laughing, groaning, scratching out, stopping to swap or share, writing again, calling for help.

And you, the teacher, are there to...

- Inspire and jog ideas from their lodging places, and keep the assignment alive and fresh.

- Listen and probe and suggest.

- Show them how to collect impressions on their own.

  Cindy ... close your eyes ... you're looking right into the wave ... see? It's coming toward you ... What is the water doing? ... What do you see in the wave? ... How does it look? ... What are the sounds? ... What do you feel against your face? ... What do you feel inside?...

- Help them find a form to fit the topic.

  You've collected a lot of memories you want to share about your dad. Could you maybe bring in some snapshots of him and combine your words with the pictures to make a photo essay?

  Jana, it sounds as if you're worried because your family hasn't sold the house yet. How about writing a real estate listing describing all the assets of your home?

- Ask open-ended questions.

  What sounds would you hear in a haunted house?
  How cold was it on the ice rink?
  What thoughts did the boy have while he was lost?
  What happened to make it an awful trip?
  How does it feel to be the youngest person in a large group?
  Who else was around?

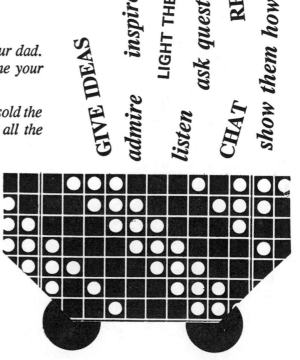

- Read, admire, chat, encourage. Praise genuinely and specifically.

  Brett, these words make my stomach feel like it's on a rollercoaster!

  Shane … liquid dancing is a wonderful phrase for this spot!

- Watch for those who need help. Give them more ideas, combine them with other writers, or invite them to write with you.

- Support their revision attempts.

  That was a wise change. It adds more mystery.
  Frantic was a good replacement—it says so much more than worried.
  This was a great improvement to combine these two sentences … it's so much smoother now.

- Write along with them. Once it looks as if writers are started, sit down and write yourself. Keep squeezing in your own writing between forays out to help kids. **Nothing transforms the writing atmosphere quite like this act—the teacher writing with the students.** Why? because it speaks so loudly for the importance and fulfillment of writing. It also puts you right on their level as a writer. You are being as open and vulnerable and eager to learn and grow as you're asking them to be. And beyond that, they love to hear your rough drafts. They're thrilled to get a chance to offer opinions and revisions to you, and kids do enjoy your finished products.

What a nice partnership in the writing classroom—teacher and kids engaged together! It's a delightfully chaotic setting! You're there to light the fire and keep it fueled. The kids add the sizzle and the crackle.

"BUT THAT ALL TAKES SO MUCH TIME," YOU'RE SAYING!

YES ... BUT ... How much time do you give daily to reading and math? Isn't writing as important a life skill?

ALSO... If you're frustrated because it takes so many days to write and edit and revise and share stories or long pieces ... try short forms. Who says long pieces are the only important writing? A class can collect and tell favorite jokes, examine the structure and language of many jokes to see what makes them funny, brainstorm ideas for jokes and collect hilarious situations or punchlines, split into pairs and write some, read them to partners, gather in small groups for responding and editing and checking mechanics, revise them and post them in a GIGGLE GALLERY ... all in a 50-minute period.

BESIDES... Writing is a process ... so it needn't always start and finish in one lesson. Spread an experience over a few days. Come back to a form later ... build and refine. OR, just pick one stage to work on at a time. For instance, GIVE kids a rough draft, and let them work in small groups to do stages 6 and 7—the responding and revising.

FURTHERMORE... Writing isn't something that has to be squeezed into writing period or English class or language arts block. Writing knows no subject-area bounds. Think of writing instruction as something that happens also when kids are...

... describing the outcome of a science experiment.
... reviewing understandings about exercise in physical education.
... explaining a problem solution in math.
... sharing a mini-biography of a composer in music.
... summarizing a historical novel for social studies.
... designing a healthy eating plan for health class.
... giving an evaluative response to a piece of artwork
... or...

AND ANYWAY... Writing is **always** a wise use of time ... and not only because writing is a process and includes many valuable skills. When kids work with the writing process, they are not just learning to write. They're reinforcing reading, speaking, and other language skills. They're developing dozens of thinking skills. They're organizing and evaluating. They're integrating many areas of learning. They're sharing and collaborating with other human beings. **And** they're building self-confidence.

PAINTED WRITING: A SAMPLE LESSON THROUGH ALL 10 STAGES

(This sample lesson is a collaboration by a 4th grade class—but this is an idea which works nicely for all ages of kids and grownups.)

STAGE 1
MOTIVATION

10 minutes

The teacher showed the class several examples of painted writing—sentences, prose, and poems in which words were placed on the paper in a way so as to suggest or look like the subject...

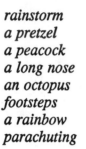

a slithery snake...an ocean wave...lightning...fire

Then students suggested other topics for painted writing...

rainstorm	pole vaulting	an octopus	a layered sandwich	a flock of birds
a pretzel	a tornado	an eraser	crawling snails	a giraffe
a peacock	a sunset	a blizzard	sky writing	skateboarding
a long nose	a juggler	a skier	a bouncing ball	a cricket
an octopus	trampolinist	a lollipop	walking on stilts	a pogo stick
footsteps	roller coaster	a ghost	falling leaves	an earthquake
a rainbow	fireworks	home run	melting ice cream	a hula hoop
parachuting	a pesky fly	tennis	mountain climbing	windstorm

STAGE 2
COLLECTING
IMPRESSIONS

10 minutes

The group chose *fireworks* as a theme for their collaborative effort. The teacher asked, *"What actions do you experience as you watch and hear and feel fireworks? Let's make a list of action words."* Students brainstormed LIST 1.

Next, the teacher asked, *"What colors do your see when you watch fireworks?"* Students generated words on **LIST 2** from their own ideas and from use of reference books such as a thesaurus, the class word collection book, and an encyclopedia.

Next, the teacher asked, *"Suppose you've never even heard of fireworks, but all of a sudden you see them. What might be happening to cause all that noise and all those colors in the sky?"* Students suggested ideas for **LIST 3**.

LIST 1

burn
sprinkle
shoot
drip
crack
light up
explode
fling
hurry
pop
burst
split
spray
crack
splatter
thunder
shatter
opening
sparkle
unfolding
dripping

LIST 2

gold
fluorescent
purple
kaleidoscope
silver
green
red
sunshine yellow
emerald
crimson
fuchsia
violet
hues
black
sky
azure
orange
bright
orchid
brilliant
turquoise

LIST 3

painting the sky
rainbow at night
raining fire
throwing out colors
jets making streaks
colored popcorn
a surprise party
a colored fan
patterns in the sky

clouds are exploding
dripping colors on the trees
spraying colored water
bright confetti in the air
colored octopus arms (tentacles)
particles (fragments) flying
someone making colored designs
a paintbox bursting open
turning on lights in the sky

LIGHTNING SCRATCHES THE SKY WITH FORKED FINGERS. IT REACHES DOWN AND CLAWS THE GROUND.

STAGE 3 **ORGANIZING**	Students began grouping some words and ideas together in a chart form, with the aid of teacher questions such as:

5 minutes

*Which color would you fit with **streak**?*

*Which action goes well with the **fan** idea?*

*What might you combine with **splatter**?*

*What color fits with **exploding into the clouds**?*

STAGE 4 **ROUGH DRAFT**	The groups of ideas from stage 3 were expanded into complete lines for a poem.

10 minutes

In the group process, students suggested lines or phrases which others expanded. The teacher recorded lines in a list on the chalkboard as they were contributed:

Drip orchid over the trees
Turn on lights in the sky
Paint the space with brilliant colors
Streak gold across the sky
Rain azure drops of fire
Shoot forth crimson tentacles
Open up a purple fan
Sprinkle fluorescent popcorn
Spray the night with emerald
Explode orange into the clouds
Burst open a turquoise surprise
Fling fuchsia fragments
Splatter the dark with hues
Light up the world with chartreuse
Crack and pop and split the night
Shatter the grey night

In this stage, take whatever ideas students give—they can be amended or eliminated later. Encourage everyone to contribute at least one line. Do this quickly and get lots of possible lines that you can work with in future stages of the process.

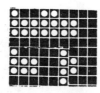

**STAGE 5
AUTHOR'S
REVIEW**

When working together with a group, this stage becomes merged with Stage 6, **Sharing for Response**, because all students are the authors.

5 minutes

During this group experience, two kids volunteered to read the draft aloud while the class listened. The teacher asked students to listen for certain strengths and weaknesses that would help with the next two stages, **response** and **revision**....

... lines that were repetitive

... lines that had pleasing sounds or combinations of words that seemed **just right**

... obviously missing words

... rough, uneven, or awkward sounding lines

... lines that sounded incomplete

... words out of order

... missing ideas

STAGE 6
SHARING
for RESPONSE

Students were invited and encouraged to respond to the rough draft with praises and suggestions. The teacher elicited responses from students by asking questions such as...

10 minutes
Stages 6/7

Which lines do you like just the way they are?
Which lines sound interesting?
Are there any lines that are too much alike?
Are there any lines that seem ordinary and could be made more interesting?
Should any lines be dropped?
Which words are best at bringing a picture to your mind? Can you add others that do this?
Which words are most interesting or effective?
Do you see any words that might be replaced with more active or more colorful ones?
Are there any good ideas that we left out?
How shall the poem begin? Is there a good beginning line here, or do we need to add something?
Is there a good ending line?
Should we rearrange the lines for better sound?
Can you suggest an order for the lines?

116

**STAGE 7
EDITING &
REVISING**

As the group was responding with comments, additions, and suggestions, one student noted changes on the rough draft copy on the overhead projector. The responses from Stage 6 resulted in a consensus to make the following revisions which include word changes, additions of lines and words, reordering of lines...

1 *Firecracker, firecracker*
2 *Hurry to the end of your fuse*
                                    and
7 *Drip orchid over the trees*

  Turn on lights in the sky
       universe
3 *Paint the ~~space~~ with brilliant colors*

5 *Streak gold across the sk~~y~~ies*

8 *Rain azure drops of fire*

9 *Shoot forth crimson tentacles*
  Unfold   *shimmering*
11 *~~Open up~~ a purple fan*

12 *Sprinkle fluorescent popcorn in pretty*
         summer   *patterns*
4 *Spray the night with emerald*

14 *Explode orange into the clouds*

10 *Burst open a turquoise surprise*

13 *Fling fuchsia fragments*

   Splatter the dark with hues
         heavens
6 *Light up the ~~world~~ with chartreuse*
                              silence
15 *Crack and pop and split the ~~night~~*

16 *Shatter the grey night*

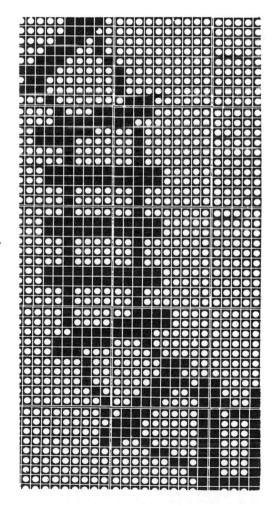

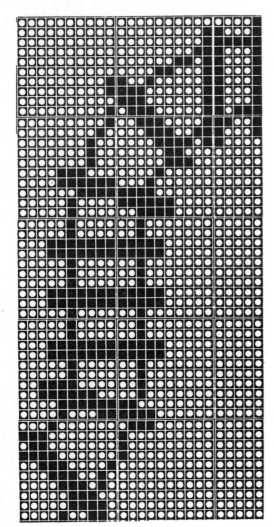

STAGE 8
MECHANICS
CHECK

10 minutes

Everyone re-read the edited draft to search for spelling and structural errors. Some students consulted dictionaries. Some asked the teacher for suggestions and help. Together the group decided how to punctuate each line.

STAGE 9
FINAL COPY

20 minutes

Two students agreed to work at copying the revised poem onto a large piece of posterboard. They used a fat marker to carefully print the lines so that the shape of the writing would give the appearance of a fireworks display.

STAGE 10
PRESENTING

Another two students added bright-colored chalk lines and designs to strengthen visually the image of **fireworks**.

On another day, individuals wrote and designed other painted writing, following the same process used in the group piece.

Then all the finished examples of **painted writing** were displayed in the school foyer. Above the display students hung a huge paintbrush and palette (filled with color words rather than colors) and a sign saying *Writers Paint With Words*.

Note: *With painted writings, I suggest that you not even hint at the idea of adding color or DRAWING to the piece until the words are first written on the paper in the shape of the topic. Otherwise, students of all ages tend to draw a picture first and "smush" the words into the illustration. The final product is far more effective, as is the process, if the words play the central role in creating the visual form.*

Whole group time = 60 minutes not including re-printing and adding color to the final copy

118

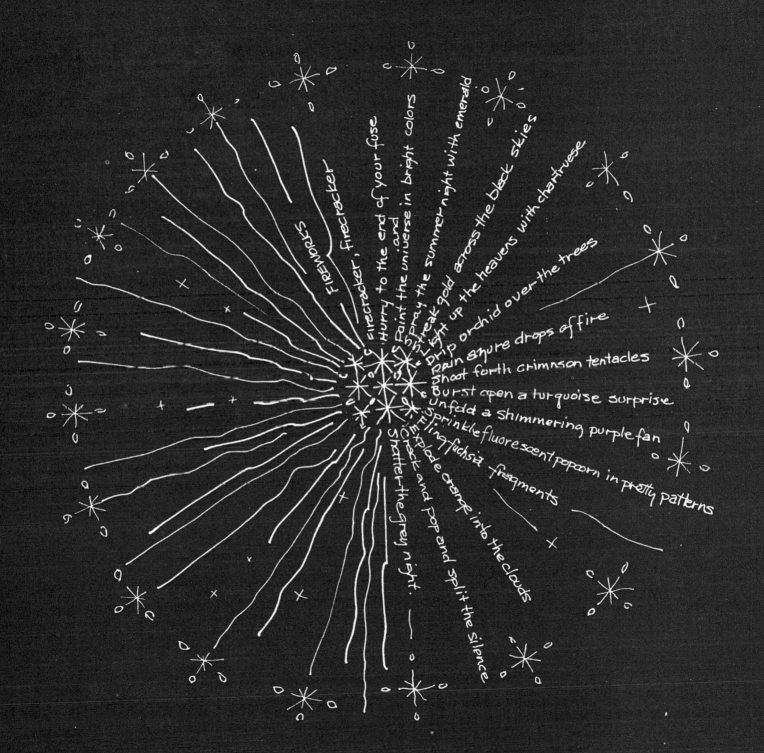

FIREWORKS

Firecracker, firecracker

Hurry to the end of your fuse
and
Paint the universe in bright colors
Spray the summer night with amber
Streak gold across the black skies
Light up the heavens with chartreuse
Drip orchid over the trees
Rain azure drops of fire
Shoot forth crimson tentacles
Burst open a turquoise surprise
Unfold a shimmering purple fan
Sprinkle fluorescent popcorn in pretty patterns
Spilling fuchsia fragments
Crack and pop and split the silence
Explode orange into the clouds
Shatter the grey night.

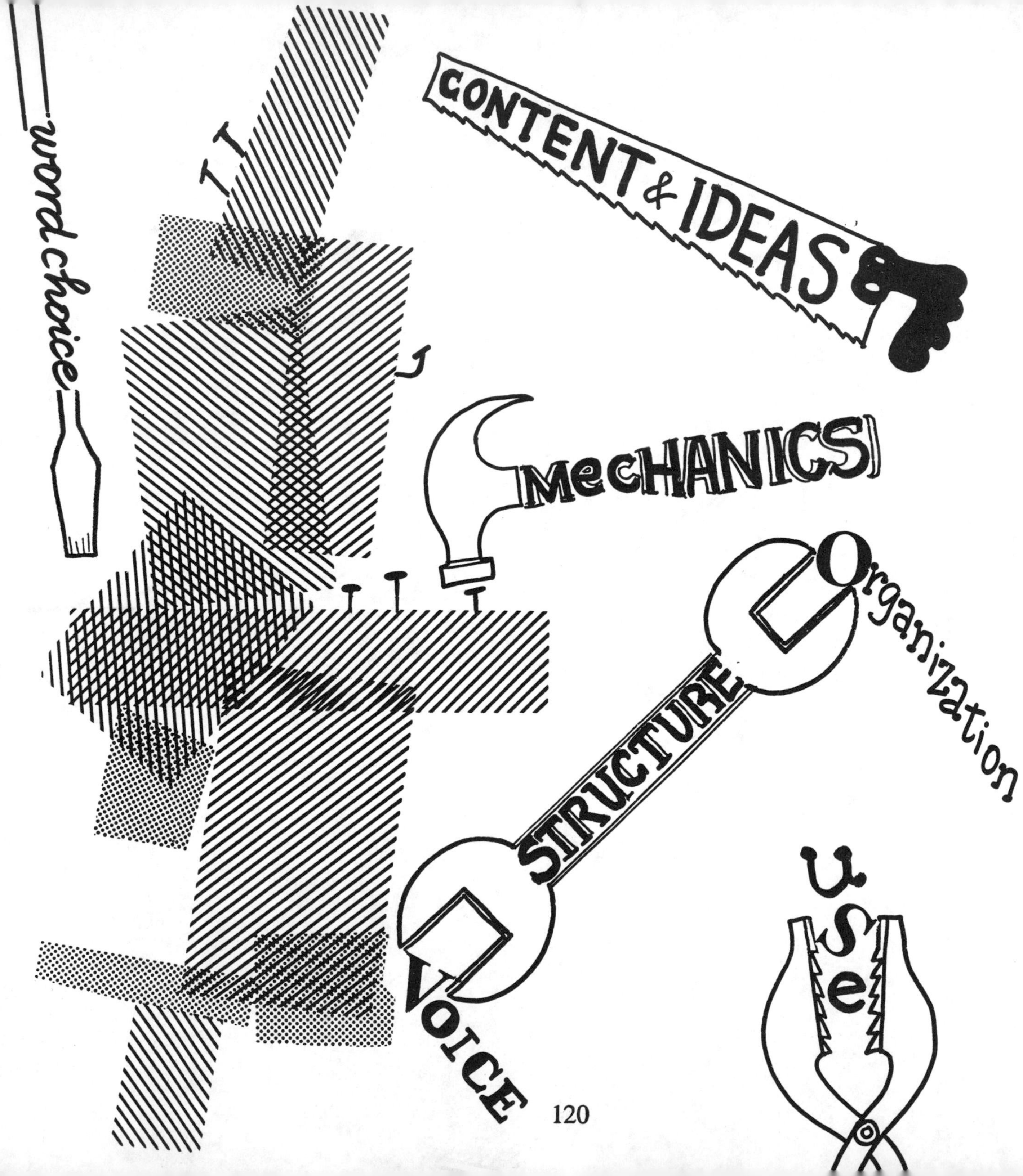

word choice

CONTENT & IDEAS

MECHANICS

Organization

STRUCTURE

VOICE

USe

5

TOOLS & TECHNIQUES

"If I focus on teaching skills, won't I stifle creativity?"

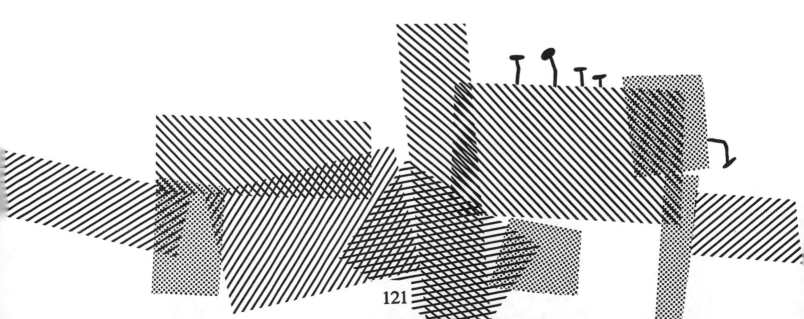

THE CREATIVITY—WRITING SKILLS TUG-OF-WAR

When someone I meet finds out that I've written books on writing, nine times out of ten that person asks me something like this...

"What kind of writing... creative writing or serious writing?"
Sometimes they actually say...

"... creative writing or real writing?"

And in gatherings of adults, when the topic of kids and writing comes up, the discussion almost always contains these opinions...

My kids write all the time in school. Their stories are great, but the spelling and grammar are atrocious!

Why don't teachers just teach basic writing skills?

Oh, just let kids write. Correcting errors just stifles imagination.

During creative writing they should be allowed to write anything any way they want. But for serious writing, accuracy is important.

All this creativity stuff is a waste. Teachers today are just too lazy to teach real writing skills.

Creativity is more important than spelling.

Well I don't care about imagination. I want my kids to be able to write decent sentences. Otherwise they'll never make it to college.

Yes, many adults, including teachers, separate the tools of writing from the content, *"serious"* writing from imaginative writing, expository writing from creative writing, and writing skills from free expression. They see not only a separation—but a competition between these factors ... a competition for importance, validity, and classroom time.

BIAS #14
THERE IS NO REAL RIVALRY
BETWEEN SKILLS AND CREATIVITY

Good writing is based on a healthy friendship between imagination and technique. It can and must be taught without slighting either.

The rivalry exists only in the minds of people who haven't thought much about the true nature of the writing process. Good teachers have always known that the freedom to wonder and experiment is crucial for learning to write. They've also known that, for any writer, there comes a time when he must simply sit on the chair, pick up the pen and write to perfect the message. They know about the marriage of inspiration and discipline in good writing.

All writing is original or creative to some degree. There's no good reason to separate *creative* from *non-creative* writing. Any time a student writes a question, an explanation, an analysis, an essay answer to a social studies question, a journal entry, she's creating—as surely as if she were inventing a myth. And then, even the most inventive writing has to cope with structure and sequencing of sentences, careful word choice, paragraph organization, and place-ment of punctuation.

Originality ... creativity ... whatever you call it ... goes hand in hand with the technical skills of writing. Creative thinking is a component of most writing skills. And it takes technical skills to be able to bring a creative idea to life in words. Chapters 5 and 6 are all about teaching kids to use these skills to make their writing effective.

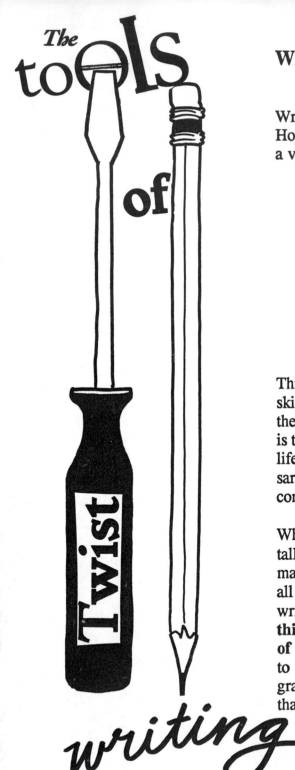

The tools of

Twist

writing

WHAT ARE THE TOOLS OF WRITING?

Writing tools are the various **skills** a writer needs for the craft. Hopefully, as writers learn and grow, they will become familiar with a variety of tools and get better at using them effectively.

> ### BIAS #15
> ### THE TOOLS ARE NOT THE WRITING
>
> *Writing tools, mechanical or otherwise, are necessary for effective writing, but, by themselves, do not communicate. It is the way the tools are used by the writer that makes the message clear or powerful. Teachers and students must take care not to confuse the tools with the writing.*

This is a chapter that emphasizes the importance of writing tools, or skills. But I'm going to tell you that teaching about the tools is not the most important task for you. Why not? Your most important job is to teach writers. Without the writer, the writing techniques have no life ... no meaning ... no use. Oh yes, writing skills are good. Necessary. You'll work with them daily. But think of them only in the context of working with living, human writers.

When I mention *writing skills* to teachers, they often assume that I'm talking about *the mechanical skills of writing (conventions)*. This may not be as true as it was 15 years ago, and it may not be true at all for you now. But for many, for a long time, when we reviewed writing or thought about helping kids work on their writing—**the first thing that got our attention was the correctness (or incorrectness) of mechanics.** Isn't that right? When we asked kids to proofread or to make corrections, weren't we primarily talking about spelling, grammar, punctuation, paragraphing, completeness of sentences? Isn't that what we ... and our students ... thought needed fixing?

Thank goodness, we have a broader view of what writing skills are now. Let's hope that old habit of being loose with the red pen and circling every mechanical error is dying out forever. Working with process writing and performance assessments has opened many teachers up to the awareness that conventions are **only one** kind of tool that helps writers communicate.

So what are these skills of writing that get used as tools by writers? There are many. Different writing systems laid out by different "experts" provide different categories and labels. But generally, writing skills touch on areas such as...

> content or ideas
> word use and choice
> overall flow, sense, or readability
> voice
> organization
> sentence sense, use, and structure
> mechanics (or conventions)

Within each of these categories, several skills could be isolated, of course. If you want kids to develop good organization in writing, you won't tackle it all at once in one big lump. You'll pay attention to what your writers need and introduce a variety of appropriate techniques to them over time to help strengthen their writing.

The pages that follow identify many specific writing skills that writers of various abilities and ages can use to assist their expression. **Mechanical skills** are separated out for discussion on pages 128-129.

Then, Chapter 6 gives a more detailed plan for introducing and strengthening these writing skills as you work with the response and revision stages of the writing process.

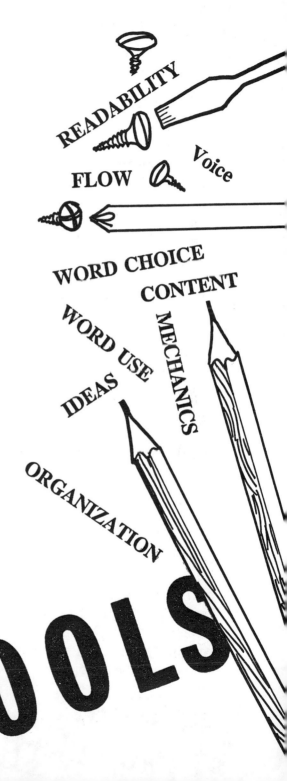

READABILITY

FLOW Voice

WORD CHOICE
CONTENT
WORD USE
MECHANICS
IDEAS
ORGANIZATION

TOOLS

SOME SKILLS FOR BEGINNING WRITERS...

Using words that readers can understand
Choosing words that bring a picture to the reader's mind
Choosing strong words
Choosing specific words
Including active words
Including colorful or unusual words
Using a variety of words
Using words and phrases that create a certain mood
Arranging words within a sentence for an interesting sound
Arranging words within sentences in different ways
Arranging words to make the idea or sentence clear
Writing sentences that make sense
Including details
Presenting ideas that are clear, not muddled
Expanding phrases into sentences
Using examples to show something
Arranging sentences within a piece for proper sequence
Arranging sentences within a piece for clarity
Arranging sentences within a piece for a good sound
Writing sentences of different lengths
Using a variety of sentences (statements, exclamations, questions)
Varying sentence beginnings so they don't all start the same
Creating exciting beginnings
Making strong endings
Making sure a piece has a beginning, middle, and end
Using similes and metaphors
Using simple rhymes
Using simple dialogue
Creating interesting and appropriate titles
Writing for a particular audience
Putting your own personality or flavor (voice) into your writing
Trying different forms: persuading, explaining, story-telling,
   imagining, describing

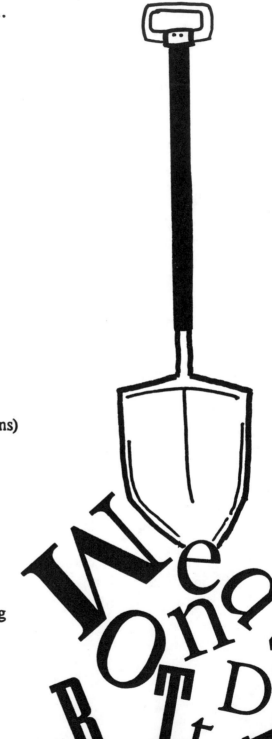

126

SOME SKILLS FOR EXPERIENCED WRITERS...

Using effective words (specific, unusual, colorful, active, etc)
Using active rather than inactive words
Choosing words that produce strong visual images
Avoiding repetitive words, phrases, ideas, sentences
Avoiding unnecessary words, phrases, ideas, sentences
Avoiding overused words, phrases and cliches
Including detail in sentences
Arranging words within sentences for clarity
Arranging words within sentences for interesting sound
Creating pieces that move along logically
Creating pieces that have strong beginning, middle, and end
Making strong connections between ideas or parts of the piece
Supplying plenty of interesting, relevant details and examples
Using enough examples to support the main idea well
Including details that are surprising, unusual, or extraordinary
Arranging sentences for proper sequence
Creating sentences with interesting rhythm
Creating sentences and paragraphs that are fluent
Creating strong endings
Creating smashing beginnings
Creating strong titles
Adapting form, style, or content for a specific purpose
Adapting form, style, or content for a specific audience
Choosing words, phrases, and style to create a certain mood
Varying sentence length
Varying sentence structure
Using dialogue
Including literary techniques such as understatement, exaggeration,
    irony, foreshadowing
Creating pieces with a particular bias
Infusing personal flavor (VOICE) into the piece
Developing use of various writing modes
Experimenting with many different forms of writing

ABOUT MECHANICS...

If a student knows that her writing will be evaluated with heavy emphasis on...

spelling
punctuation
sentence structure
grammar and usage
punctuation
capitalization

she will probably...

use only words she's sure she can spell
interrupt her thinking process to ask about spelling
interrupt her thinking process to worry about mechanics
keep sentences simple to avoid making mistakes
avoid any unusual punctuation situations
stick to ordinary sentence structure
write shorter, less complete pieces

... all of which adds up to NO risk, NO stretching, LITTLE growth, and even LESS excitement or discovery.

If a student has the freedom to write and write and write...

knowing he can go back later to change and correct
knowing he'll have help with the fixing
knowing his ideas are more important than mechanics
knowing he'll not be branded *slow* or *a poor writer* if he's got mistakes to fix in the reworking

... then he can really let his ideas flow ... try out possibilities ... take the chances that will lead to real growth in his writing.

SO...

- **Spare the red pen!** Instead...
  Make your suggestions on a separate scrap of paper or attach a sticky note with your responses. Keep a card file or notebook, noting misspelled words for each student. (Add them to next week's spelling list.) Hold quick conferences with individuals or small groups to locate errors. Or get some volunteer parents, grandparents, or older students to help with editing.

- **Teach the kids to do the checking.**
  With the whole group, identify and correct structural or mechanical problems. Then give correcting tasks to students in pairs or small editing groups...

  How many run-on sentences can your editing group find?
  Take 3 minutes to check for proper punctuation of quotes.

- **Identify mechanical skills and include them.**
  Make a list of the skills needed at your grade level. Emphasize these skills in regular instruction or plan mini-lessons during language class. Then watch for chances to reinforce those skills, one at a time, during writing sessions.

- **Return to those skills in later writing.**
  Once they've repaired mistakes of one kind, make use of that learning in future writing ... preferably soon!

  Today when you write, BEWARE of run-on sentences.

- **Talk about mistakes as a normal part of the process.**
  Make it clear that writers work constantly with dictionaries and grammar books—that fixing is just part of writing!

You'll find that your students can become good fixers of their own material ... if you work on one skill at a time. As they gain experience in editing, they begin to care more. Mechanics become important to a polished piece, and **kids actually ask for help.**

NURTURING WRITING SKILLS

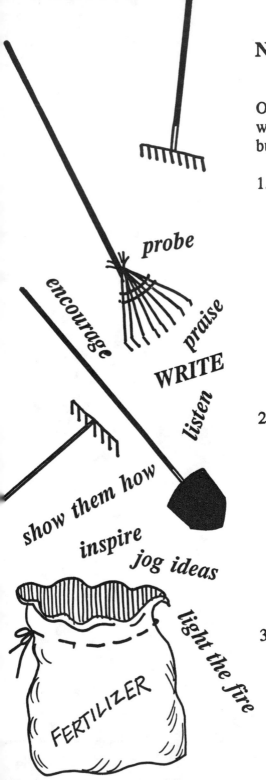

Okay, so there are enough writing tools to keep teachers and young writers busy and growing for years. How do you work them into the business of building writers? Here are a few ways that I like...

1. **Visit separate writing skills within regular language lessons.**

   Lots of this stuff is right there—within your English text, your reading program, your language arts instruction. Don't miss an opportunity to do activities—separate from your writer's workshop or writing sessions—that teach and reinforce such things as...
   varying sentence structure
   putting ideas into sequence
   using examples to support ideas
   learning and using effective new words
   and so on...

2. **Re-visit those language skills during writing sessions.**

   I'll lobby any day for teaching separate, well-planned activities concentrating on language skills. But I believe we're being dishonest with students if we teach skills in the morning language arts period and then, during afternoon writing class, say, *"Never mind that stuff."* The writing setting is too fine an opportunity for strengthening and making relevant those tools to be leaving them out. Constantly refresh and remind students about the skills they've learned in other classes, other parts of the curriculum, other times of the day.

3. **Sneak little lessons into individual writing conferences.**

   Much of your best help to writers at any stage of the process happens naturally when you (or a mentor or a writing partner) sit with a student to enjoy and respond to a rough draft of a written piece. Use this time to gently and **briefly** teach a skill.

130

4. **Plan mini-lessons on specific writing skills.**

When you plan your writing instruction or writer's workshop or class writing period, include some time to stop and concentrate on specific skills. Choose a skill that fits the genre your group is working with, a skill that your writers have been stumbling over, or a skill you think they need to practice. **Be sure to keep these MINI!** My daughter complains regularly that her writing teacher uses up the whole writing period every day with his *mini* lessons ... and then the kids never have time left to write! Try mini-lessons on these topics or skills from pages 126-127.

SUGGESTED MINI-LESSON TOPICS

- planning a piece of writing
- getting ideas organized
- specific kinds of writing
- specific modes of writing
- replacing weak words with stronger or more interesting words
- writing for a specific audience
- good sequence, sense of storyline
- strengthening voice
- paragraphs that "work"
- putting poetry into lines effectively
- rearranging or expanding or changing sentences to make them effective
- adding details and examples
- eliminating repetitive ideas/words
- eliminating unnecessary ideas/words
- selecting words to set a mood
- writing to accomplish a purpose
- using a variety of sentences
- strong beginnings
- strong endings
- effective middles
- good titles
- replacing inactive with active words
- using metaphors, exaggeration, figures of speech, humor, irony
- clarity of ideas
- using dialogue
- varying rhymes and rhythms
- increasing reader appeal
- improving transitions
- varying punctuation
- separating facts from opinions
- adding or eliminating bias

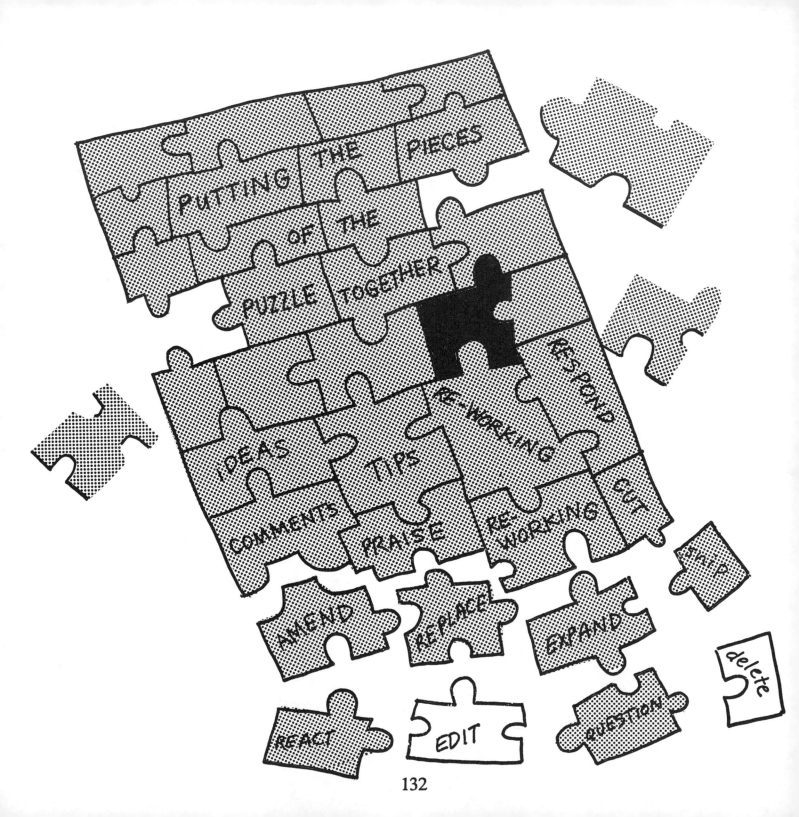

PUTTING THE PIECES OF THE PUZZLE TOGETHER

IDEAS   TIPS   RE-WORKING   RESPOND

COMMENTS   PRAISE   RE-WORKING   CUT

REACT   EDIT   QUESTION   delete

AMEND   REPLACE   EXPAND

132

6

RESPONSE & REVISION

"It's like pulling teeth to get kids to edit and revise!"

What Is Response?
What Is Revision?
Response & Revision...The Two Go Together
The P-Q-P Plan For Responding And Revising
Tips For Teaching Kids How To Respond To Writing
Tips For Teaching Kids How To Revise Writing

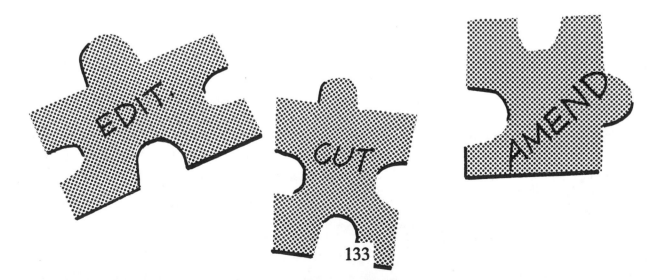

133

WHAT IS RESPONSE?

TO RESPOND: to react to something

Reacting—that's just what happens in Stage 5 of the Writing Process. The writer listens to (or reads or otherwise takes in) **reactions** to the writing. This may be in the form of comments, praises, advice, tips, questions, suggestions, ideas. It may come from peers, the teacher, parents, students in other classes, or any number of other sources—and, of course, from the writer herself or himself.

Writers NEED to gather reactions to their writing. They NEED to give responses to others' writing. This is how they think about and talk about and grow in their understanding of...

... what works, what doesn't, what might work better.

... what makes sense, what doesn't.

... what is strong, effective, confusing, ordinary, surprising, striking.

... how the writing affects the audience.

Unfortunately, response is too often shortchanged in classrooms. Writers go from the rough draft straight to revision! Right? You've seen this, haven't you? You've probably done it. I used to ... all the time. It usually happens like this. After the draft...

> The teacher reads the writing, marks errors, and directs students about what revisions to make.

> ### OR

> The teacher directs students to go back through the piece on their own to revise, sometimes with a written editing guide.

Let's all get off the non-stop track from draft to revision, and spend some time wandering around looking for responses before settling in to revise. **This is a crucial stage to improving the craft of writing.** Don't move on without it!

134

WHAT IS REVISION?

TO REVISE: *to amend, correct, or improve*

The writer has reviewed the work looking for ways to improve it and has gathered responses from others. Now it's time to get down to the job of deciding what needs to be done to this piece of writing … and then doing it: rearranging, expanding, deleting, adding. This includes anything from reshuffling or replacing words, phrases, or sentences to reworking the whole piece.

REVISION—the stage with the bad reputation. The one that leaves writers grumbling and teachers trembling. It seems to produce the most anxiety and least enthusiasm of any part of the writing process. **Why?** Well, to be truthful, revision does take work. But I don't believe that's the whole reason so many writers and teachers find it uncomfortable or even reprehensible. I believe revision is so painful because we've been asked to do it without being taught how. Writers **think** it's going to be hard before they even start it, because they haven't been eased into doing it with lots of tools or help.

For years, I consistently (and conscientiously) asked my students, *"Did you proofread and revise your paper?" "Oh, yes, Mrs. Frank,"* was usually the immediate response. I must have read a thousand of those papers before I faced the reality that their editing (if indeed they did it at all) was mostly in vain. How could they revise when I had not shown them how? Oh, I had edited **for** them on occasion or taught them a few things to "fix." But I had not taught them clearly about specific writing skills and how to use them or improve them.

The goal of revision, of course, is to polish the writing in some way. The writer gains the experience of improving writing and, at the same time, feels the satisfaction of having grown as a writer. This is what we give to our writers when we take the time to provide meaningful responses to their writing and help them learn to revise their work.

RESPONSE and REVISION ... THE TWO GO TOGETHER

> **BIAS #16**
> **RESPONSE MAKES or BREAKS THE REVISION**
> *Without feedback about the strengths and needs of the writing, the author has no real substance to take along to the task of revising the piece.*

I've described **response** and **revision** separately here, in order to explain them clearly. But actually, I believe they are inseparable.

... If you don't know what is effective in your writing, how do you know what to keep?

... If you have no idea what is confusing, how can you clear it up?

... If no audience lets you know about the voice in your writing, how can you tell if it's strong or weak?

... If one idea makes sense and another doesn't but you haven't figured it out on your own ... how do you know to eliminate one?

Response drives the revision. It is the raw material the writer uses to think about the work and make decisions about what to keep, what to drop, what to change.

But also, revision feeds response. As writers take input and work with it, they become better at giving response in the future. Hearing suggestions, thinking about them, putting them to work to make writing better (whether in their own work or someone else's) ... all this nurtures their abilities to think about and respond to writing.

You'll see it happen! The more kids respond ... the better they'll revise. The more kids revise ... the better they'll become at giving insightful and helpful responses. You'll also see that it is the interplay of response and revision that really improves writing.

Teachers, beware of this temptation:

... doing the responding for them (being the main person who reflects back what is good and weak about a piece of writing).

... AND/OR doing the revising for them (telling students what they should eliminate, add, or change).

It's one of the big mistakes teachers make when writing with kids. Avoid it at all costs. The whole purpose for teaching the writing process to kids is to build writers. Kids will never think of themselves as real writers unless they do **all** parts of the process for themselves.

I have to confess that, for years, I spent very little time helping kids learn to respond and revise. It's not that I didn't love writing. It's not that I was an irresponsible teacher. Partly, it was that I didn't know how important these were to improving writing. Partly, there was a lack of time. Partly, I wasn't too secure in my ability to do this. But mostly, I suffered from disbelief. I didn't really believe that kids, especially little kids, were capable of identifying and making the kinds of improvements they needed to make in their writing—certainly not as well as I could. And was I ever wrong! I'm still embarrassed by the meagerness of my faith.

So, you're getting the idea that I believe kids can and should learn to be good at these two stages of the writing process. But I also believe this isn't likely to happen without some effective teaching. So the purpose of this chapter is to share approaches I've observed and tried that have helped writers of many ages become good at responding to writing and revising writing.

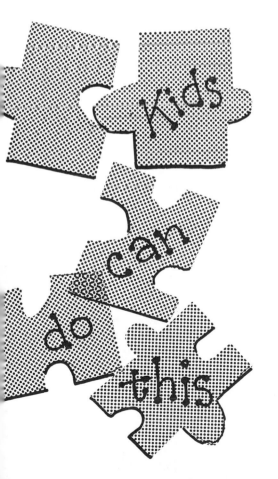

137

THE P-Q-P PLAN for RESPONDING & REVISING

So, just what can writers do with a rough draft to learn about effective writing and go on to make improvements?

Here's an easy-to-use plan you can teach your students to guide them through the response and revision stages. The first **P** and the **Q** are response tactics: **Praise** and **Question**. The last **P** is the revision tactic: **Polish**. Writers of all ages can make improvements in their writing by remembering these three steps:

PRAISE. Writers tell each other ... what's strong ... what's good ... what's effective ... what works ... what caught your ear or eye ... what's pleasing ... what sparked a thought ... what taught you something ... what surprised or delighted you ... etc.

Crash! was a great choice for the opening sentence! It grabbed my attention right away.

It was a good idea to string all those short words together in this part.

It made the girl seem very much in a hurry.

*I liked the way you repeated the **T** sound over and over in this poem. That gave a marching rhythm to the poem.*

I like the wet words for your rain poem. My favorites were slosh... slurpy...slush...drizzle...slop...and...splatter.

The ending was a great surprise. It really caught me off guard.

The part about the alligator swallowing the umbrella was my favorite!

*I like the part about the **squirmy, squishy, soft and mushy worm.***

Tom, your title "The Food No Kid Should Eat," made me want to listen to your paragraph.

It was such a good idea to end the argument with a question. That really made me question the safety of skateboards too.

These two sentences right here—really show your sense of humor.

I like the way you started the argument by telling all the good things about fast foods before you switched to your pitch against them. That gave an unusual twist and caught my attention.

138

QUESTION.

QUESTION. Writers ask questions that will help the author review and think about the writing to ... realize where things may not be clear ... hear where something is missing ... notice where something could be stronger, funnier, more suspenseful, more informative ... etc... and consider what could be changed or added or removed.

This is not harsh criticism. No outside opinion is forced on the writer. That's the reason for using the **question** form. A question is stated and left for the author to answer and decide.

Your autobiography didn't tell much about your preschool years. Could you add a few sentences about that?

How did your puppy get lost anyway?

I felt as if you gave away the ending too soon. Could you add something right here to prolong the suspense a bit?

*Could you replace the word **neat** with a different word in two of the three places you used it?*

*What would **you** have said to this reporter? What is **your** opinion about this topic? I'd like to get more of a feel for **your** voice.*

I'm confused about how the girls got into the volcano in the first place. Could you add a sentence or two to make that clear?

What color was your kitten? Was it little? How did you feel about finding her after a whole week?

*Didn't the gorilla have to escape from the zoo **before** he sat on the mayor? Shouldn't this sentence come before this one?*

*What is **your** feeling about this earthquake? I don't get much of an idea of the author's involvement in this.*

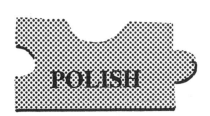

POLISH. After gaining some responses from others, the author decides what input to use ... what suggestions to discard or include ... what changes to make ... which feedback is important. And then the author adds this information to his or her own ideas to put to use in a new draft. It's unlikely that all of the responses can be used. Nor should they be. That, finally, is up to the author to decide.

TIPS FOR TEACHING KIDS HOW TO RESPOND TO WRITING

Here are some suggestions which I've found helpful for turning kids into caring, effective responders:

1. **Build a spirit of kind helpfulness.**

   When you begin the process of responding to writing, clarify that the purposes are: to support writers, build self-confidence, strengthen good writing that is being done, and increase writing skills. The aim is to build writers—not to destroy egos, criticize negatively, feel superior, or poke fun.

   Talk about feelings ... how hard it is to feel criticized, how tearing-down statements hurt, how sensitive people may be about the ideas and thoughts they've put onto paper.

   Talk about tact: about how, "*I think the ending might be funnier if...*" is easier to take than, "*The ending is dumb.*"

   Talk about how **EVERYBODY'S** writing is helped when people examine and discuss one person's work.

2. **Ease into it.**

   Start small. Have the whole group or small groups read—then respond— to just a few things. Start with anonymous pieces (things you've found, created, or saved from other years). OR let them respond to one of yours. Then gradually move towards using parts of their own writing. And finally, move to working with their whole pieces. Go back to working with short and anonymous pieces often. This is far less threatening than the close scrutiny of their own work, and kids are more likely to succeed.

3. **Start with the PRAISE.**

At the beginning ... and for a long time ... allow only **praise** responses.

Tell the author what words were most unusual.

What was strongest about the ending?

What phrase was the scariest?

Tell the author what worked best in the whole piece.

Move on to questions that might suggest change only when your writers have become very comfortable with and capable of giving and receiving praise responses.

Today, in your editing groups, compliment each author on one thing done very well and ask one question that might help the author make some improvement.

4. **Give direction for the response.**

It's a difficult task to respond to every aspect of a whole piece— for the individual writer, or for others. Teach kids to be effective responders by **suggesting** some things for them to notice.

Find the sentence that's the funniest.

Point out two words that are especially descriptive.

Are there any lines in the poem that aren't clear?

Suggest one thing that might make the tale more suspenseful.

Look for a phrase that could be made more active.

Even very young children can listen and look for one colorful word or the most exciting sentence or a line that has interesting sounds or the scariest phrase.

You won't need to **tell** kids what to look for and heavily direct their responses forever. Quite quickly, they will grow into doing this without your frequent or strong direction.

141

5. **Be specific in the response.**

Writing is a practical life skill, a tool for communicating. So give the praises and ask the questions that stretch thinking and make right-to-the-point suggestions which will improve this writing **and the next, and many more pieces to come.**

As you are working with pieces of writing, **model** the kinds of feedback that is helpful. And gently **coax** students toward responses that are specific.

For instance, comments such as these are of little help...

Lovely poem!	*Great improvement!*
That was nice.	*What a scary story!*
I liked it!	*Your jokes are funny.*
Write more.	*I don't get it.*

These, on the other hand, will make a difference...

This phrase right here was a good surprise.

The way you arranged these words made this an interesting sentence.

Could you add something to this sentence to clear up my confusion about how he got into this mess?

The name you chose for the villain was really sinister!

You chose really active and fun words to describe your puppy—it gave me an idea of how energetic she is.

Could you tell how he felt when it was all over?

How about changing the word walked to something more descriptive of the way he was walking—like stumbled?

6. **Practice responding together ... often.**

Do this in class, with the whole group or small groups. Do it a lot. Use any pieces of writing you find. Whether or not the student has written a piece, the responding experience is valuable writing instruction.

A SAUSAGE

Have you ever looked at a Sausage
A Slimy brown Sausage, a hot blunt stinky Sausage
with little pieces of grainy fat stuck in on the
sides
A gushy, green fuzzy with mold reeking Sausage
A wrinkly crinkly scaby Sausage
Have you ever looked at a Sausage?

ANNE E. LINTON

What a good idea to write about a sausage!

I like the phrase 'blunt stinky sausage!'

Yuck! I will definitely never eat sausage again.

HOT DOG!

YOU HAVE GOOD "RED" WORDS... FIRE, SPAGHETTI, CHERRY PIE, BLOOD.

RED

Red is the color of roses and noses
And cherry pie and blood.
Red is the sound of sirens and speeding police cars.
Red is being embarrassed and getting sunburned.
Red is bare feet on a hot sidewalk.
Red is Rudolph's nose and Santa's cold toes.
Red is the smell of fires or spaghetti.
I am red when someone makes fun of me.
Red is the feeling I get when my mother yells at me.

Erik, grade 3

I like the rhyme of roses and noses.

You used all 5 senses!

143

TIPS FOR TEACHING KIDS HOW TO REVISE WRITING

1. **Do it together.**

   Especially at the beginning ... especially with young writers... especially each time you try a new writing genre or work on a new technique ... especially when you begin to require more complex editing—**take the time** to lead your writers carefully through those responding-revising stages.

2. **Work with short pieces ... often!**

   Have you tried to wade through and point out all the errors and weaknesses in a 3rd grader's adventure tale or a 10th grader's ten-page autobiography? It's a bewildering task—even for a teacher—to edit such a long piece. A paragraph or two are much easier to handle in a limited time period. And short writing is much more suitable for tackling one or two areas needing improvement. Even when students go on to reworking whole pieces, come back to short ones for working on specific skills.

3. **Give direction to the revising.**

   As with the response stage, provide examples of the kinds of strengths and weaknesses to notice and revise.

   Look for sentences that don't make sense.
   Do you have a strong opening line or sentence?
   Have you begun more than three sentences with the same word?
   Try to change at least one inactive word to an active one.

4. **Practice on anonymous pieces.**

   It's less threatening and more fun to dig in and revise a piece that someone else wrote. Keep a collection of samples which kids can practice revising before they tackle their own writing.

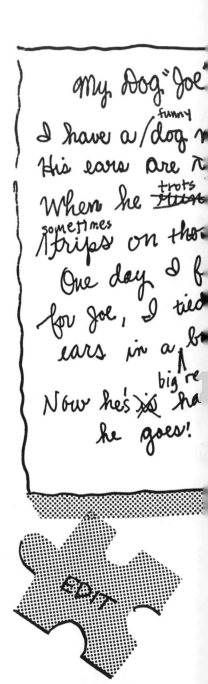

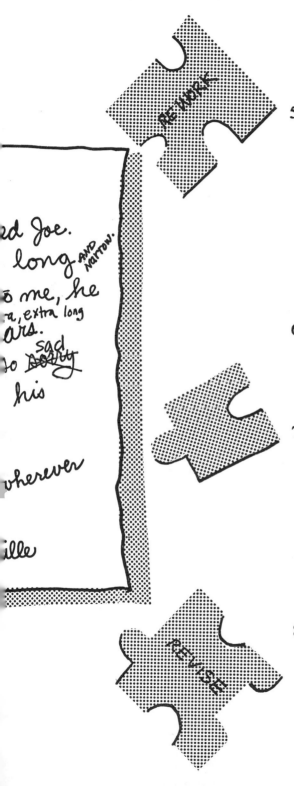

5. **Decide what techniques need to be refined.**

   Make a list of the writing problems that need to be attacked and the devices that should be strengthened. Add to this list as you watch their writing and notice other needs surfacing. Obviously, certain kinds of written forms fit best with certain writing techniques. For example, the writing of news articles is a session ready-made for working on creating smashing titles or including specific details. When the form you're working on **needs** a certain skill—that's the time it'll do the most good to work at refining it.

6. **Work on revising only a few things at a time.**

   If you're going to really improve certain writing skills, you've got to isolate them and focus on a small number at once. With many writers, it's best to only work on **one** at a time.

7. **Put the revising experience to use in the next writing.**

   Remind kids about what happened in the last writing session. That skill you practiced yesterday will improve writing tomorrow, too.

   Remember those lines from last week's city poems that were awkward because the rhyme had been forced? Let me review a few for you. Now here they are after we dropped the rhyme or rearranged the lines or concentrated on the sounds of words within lines rather than ending rhymes. When you write poetry today, try to use rhyme only when and if it doesn't confine you or spoil the meaning of the lines.

8. **Don't overdo it.**

   Kids need to learn when **not** to revise, too. If change is over-emphasized, they may start looking to tear apart everything. It isn't necessary to revise every piece of writing. You can respond to pieces and learn plenty about writing skills without going through with a full-scale revision.

Headache (draft)

A headache never has ~~a problem~~ difficulty finding a ~~good~~ home. A toothache ~~has~~ ~~must~~ ~~wait~~ for a ~~roomy~~ holey molar. An earache waits for a cold day ~~and~~ to chase ~~x~~ down hatless children. Even if an earache is lucky enough ~~and to~~ catches an ear, he has the most ~~cramped~~ quarters ~~to~~ ~~in which to live~~ ~~is~~ ~~wish must be unbearable.~~

Neither ~~a toothache nor an ear~~ ~~ache have~~ ~~that~~ as much room as I have. I don't have to ~~put~~ ~~tolerate with~~ either bad breath or sticky ~~yellow~~ ~~wax~~. I can find a home in any head ~~whenever~~ that head has a problem. (and ~~most~~ people have plenty of problems!) ~~Would you~~ ~~believe that~~ I've lived in some of the best heads! I have known movie stars, ~~presidents~~ and athletes ~~personally~~.

I've met more people than ~~almost~~ any ~~ache~~ I know, but the ~~person~~ ~~more~~ ~~I know~~ I wish I had never ~~met~~ is the ~~man~~ one who invented asprin!

Pat Gyer
Grade 8

[margin note:] And imagine how confining to be a toothache trapped inside a bicuspid!

The Advantages of Being a Headache

A headache never has difficulty finding a good home. A toothache has to hope for a vacancy in a holey molar. An earache must wait for a cold day to chase down hatless children. But I just move into a head any time.

Even if an earache is lucky enough to catch an ear, he has the most cramped quarters in which to live. And imagine how confining it is to be a toothache trapped inside a bicuspid! Neither has as much room as I. And I don't have to tolerate either bad breath or sticky yellow wax!

I can easily find lodging in any head that has a problem (and most people have plenty of problems!) Why, I've lived in some of the best heads! I've known presidents, movie stars, and even athletes, personally.

I've met more people than any other ache around, but the person I wish I'd never met is the one who invented aspirin!

Pat Gyer
Grade 8

Mud — Eddy (draft 1)

Mud

It feels so good to put your toes in slimy, gooey mud. Mud slops and plops and drops and glops. It sticks to your feet and runs through your fingers. "Goosh," goes mud. You can make mud!
mud!
mud!

Mud — Eddy (draft 2)

Mud

It feels so good to put your toes in mud. Mud slops and plops. It sticks to your feet. goosh goes mud. You can make mud!
mud!
mud!

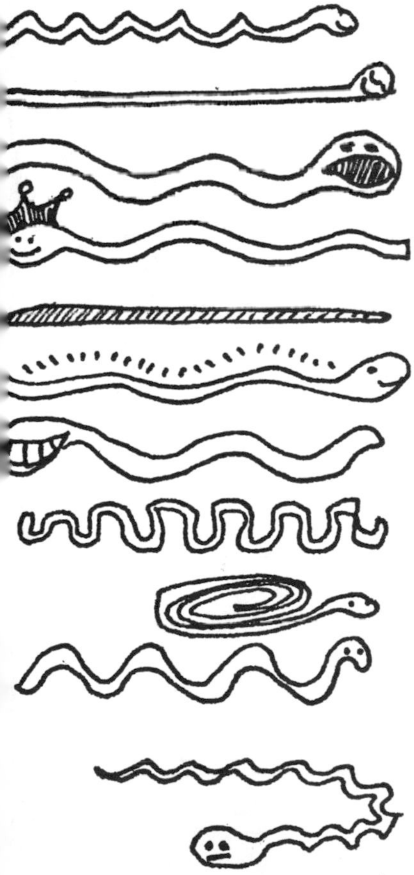

I like worms... (draft with edits)

I like worms. . .
Big worms,
Little worms,
Fast ~~Fat~~ worms,
Slow ~~Thin~~ worms,
Sassy ~~Fast~~ worms,
Flashy ~~Slow~~ worms,
Dull worms,
Glow worms —
Worms that giggle
As they ~~Worms that~~ wiggle,
Worms that curl
And Worms that hump,
Worms that scurry
In a ~~Worms that~~ hurry,
Worms that slither
Worms that slump.
One land of worm,
I say with haste,
I ~~don't much~~ Do Not like
Is a worm with taste!

I like worms... (final)

I like worms. . .
Big worms,
Little worms,
Fast worms,
Slow worms,
Sassy worms,
Flashy worms,
Dull worms,
Glow worms —
Worms that giggle
As they wiggle,
Worms that curl
And worms that hump,
Worms that scurry
In a hurry,
Worms that slither
Worms that slump.
BUT
One kind of worm,
I say with haste,
I DO NOT like
Is a worm with taste!

by Shana M.

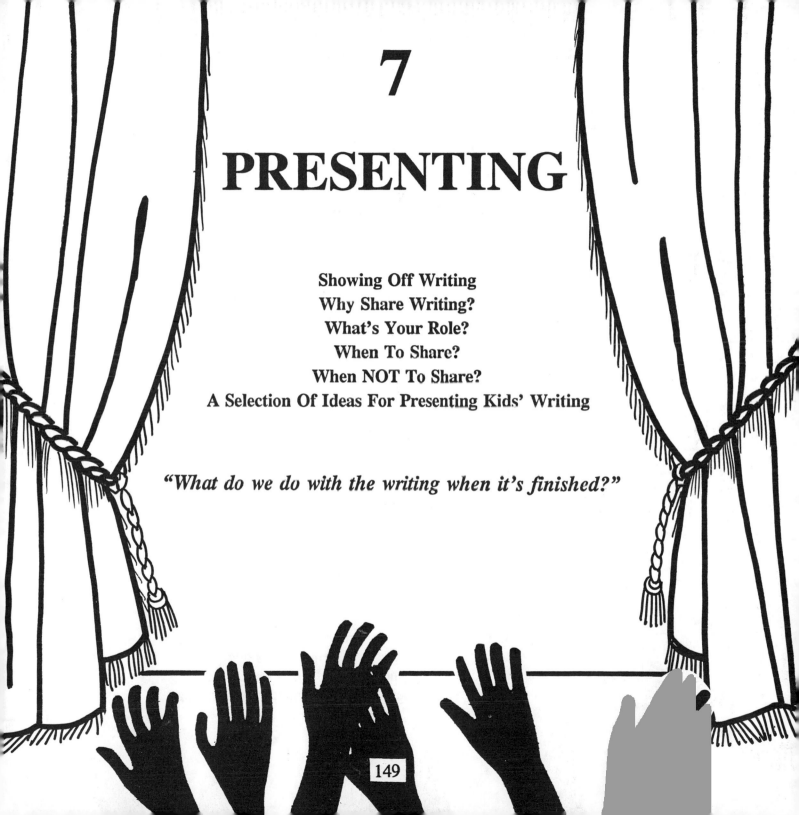

7
PRESENTING

Showing Off Writing
Why Share Writing?
What's Your Role?
When To Share?
When NOT To Share?
A Selection Of Ideas For Presenting Kids' Writing

"What do we do with the writing when it's finished?"

SHOWING OFF WRITING

> ### BIAS #18
> ### PRESENTING WRITING ADDS DIGNITY
> *Making a piece of writing public advertises the importance of the writer and the writing. Kids should have an opportunity to share EVERY finished draft, if they choose.*

WHY SHARE WRITING? Because...

Sharing IS communicating. After all ... one of the author's most compelling motivations for the labor of reworking and refining is the preparation of a personal statement for presentation to others.

Sharing gets writing out into the light. That act of presenting it ... of hearing it ... of publishing it ... of watching it live ... of seeing others' reactions to it ... provides the writer with a clearer view of the work AND influences the shape of the next work.

Sharing advances the craft of writing. If it is used as a time for pointing out effective techniques, the sharing setting is an excellent one for learning about what makes writing good ... what works ... what doesn't ... what effects certain devices produce.

Sharing increases technical accuracy. As kids write and publish they become spontaneously concerned about grammar and spelling and structure. And they begin to want to improve.

Sharing builds writers' esteem. The writer feels the fulfillment of bringing everything together into finished form. Others add positive responses. The sum total is a grand boost in self-respect. Kids see themselves as real writers, and that leads to more and better writing.

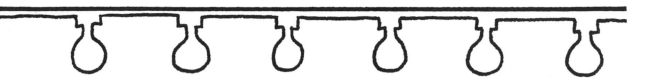

WHAT'S YOUR ROLE? As a teacher, you are there...

... **to provide the time.** Making time for them to share their writing shows students that you attach importance to it. This will increase the dignity afforded by them to their writing.

... **to treat their writing with respect.** It's a privilege if students share their personal writing with you—and they will only if they trust you as someone who listens and cares about them and their writing.

... **to use their own writing as tools and examples for advancing writing skills.** As they share, point out approaches and devices and writing techniques that make for effective writing:

Did you notice that Jim repeated the word whisper four times? What effect did that have?

This whole group looked scared when Nick read the phrase...

What words did Amanda use to create a suspenseful mood?

What feeling did you get from that whole group of very short statements that opened the monologue in Dana's play?

... **to introduce them to many modes of presenting writing.** Just "reading your story to the class" can be confining and threatening. Let your students know about enough possibilities to fit lots of different writing forms and writer personalities. Then help individuals select ways to present that fit their topics and personal styles.

151

WHEN TO SHARE?

When the writer wants to. Writers don't always want to make writing public. Nevertheless the time and means should always be available, so the writer can show off those works she feels are ready for the public.

Anytime ... Anywhere. There is no best time or one place for publishing or sharing. The locations and hours are unlimited in possibility. Both can be determined by the topic and form of the writing, as well as by the classroom schedule. Some pieces are good morning openers. Others are best saved for rainy days. There are pieces which beg to be read aloud, while others make their best impact when presented to the eyes of a single reader.

Not only when the piece is totally polished. Some of the best "sharing" times come during or after the rough draft. Always give a chance for publicizing polished pieces, but don't limit showing off to only those that are perfected either.

As soon as possible. Plan time for publicizing immediately upon finishing—while excitement is still high and the momentum of the experience surrounds the group with courage. Often the need, the bravery, and the enthusiasm for sharing wear off with too much time. Also, if you postpone publishing too long, you're shouting the message: This isn't really very important!

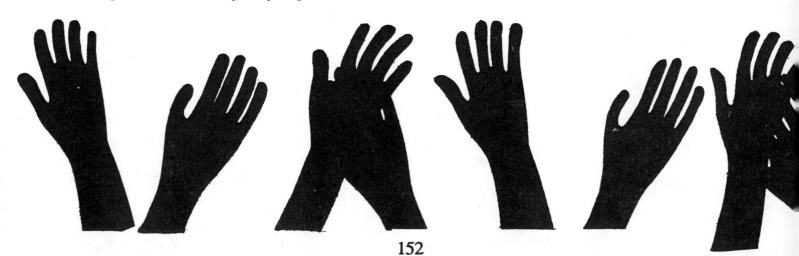

WHEN NOT TO SHARE?

Before author's private re-reading. Students should always be given the **option** of reading and revising BEFORE sharing. I can remember extreme discomfort at being commanded to read something as soon as I'd finished writing it—before I was even sure I liked it.

When a student doesn't want to. Sharing should **never** be forced. Publication is for the author to choose or refuse. I always guarantee students the privacy of any work they submit, and promise never to read anything aloud without their permission.

When there isn't sufficient time. How many times has the "sharing" part of writing gotten crammed into the last few minutes of the day or the class period. When students show off their work, make sure there is the right setting and plenty of time for them to really get the attention the writing deserves. There's nothing more disappointing than getting geared up to present your work, then having little attention or time from the audience.

However ... there certainly are some coaxing techniques for you to use when you sense that a student would like to find a way to share writing but is too shy or uncertain.

You can...

... Offer some non-threatening ways to share (ways that don't require the author to stand up in front of a group).

... Encourage the student to let you read it aloud without telling who the author is. Once he sees it accepted, he may change his mind about advertising who the author is.

... Let her "share" it with a tape recorder, some younger kids, a row of stuffed animals, or another "easy" audience.

... Create a way for private sharing such as a PRIVATE DRAWER where students may submit things without names— only for your reading.

... Help her ease into sharing by finding one person she trusts enough to begin on the "making it public" process.

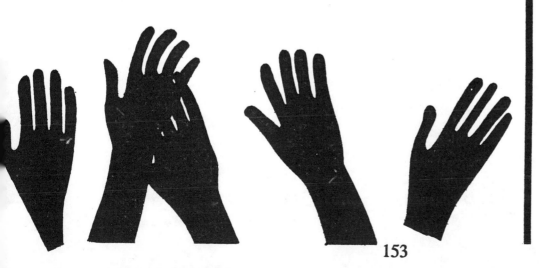

153

A SELECTION OF IDEAS FOR PRESENTING KIDS' WRITING

Wondering what to do with your writing?

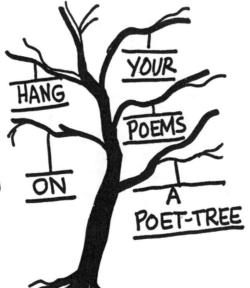

Antique it (by tearing or burning its edges).

Give readings to ...
   the custodian ...
   other classes ...
   big kids ...
   little kids ...
   the principal ...
   the cooks ...
   the mayor ...
   the School Board
   the city council
   the Chamber of Commerce
   the school nurse
   the office staff

turn it into a paper airplane. Sail it across a room

HANG IT FROM THE ♥ CEILING

MOUNT it on CARDBOARD and STAND it on an EASEL.

Mount it.

Copy it. Copy it. Copy it. Copy it.

Copy it. Copy it. Copy it. Copy it.

Create a dance to go along with it.

MAKE A PUPPET TO RECITE YOUR WRITING.

Wrap it up as a present and give it to someone special.

Print your own literary MAGAZINE or Newspaper or BOOK. Spread Your Writing ♥ Around.

≈5¢≈

Type it.

Bake it into a cookie and give it to a friend.

INSCRIBE IT IN INK ON AN OLD TEE SHIRT AND WEAR IT PROUDLY.

Build a bulletin board display around one theme using several pieces of writing and artwork.

PRINT IT IN COLOR ON LARGE SHEETS OF PAPER AND WRAP PRESENTS WITH

Write it up as a book, bind it,
cover it with fabric or wallpaper,
and donate it to your library.

Ask someone to translate it into another language.

Si, Si!

Set it to music and sing it.

Build a bulletin board display around one theme
using several pieces of writing and artwork.

Enter it into a computer. Fuss with it,
illustrate it with computer graphics, format it,
print it out in many sizes.

Send it to a literary magazine for kids.

"Write" it by pasting up cut-out letters.
Then make a rubbing of it.

FRAME IT.

Share it with a senior citizen.

Carry it to someone in a hospital or nursing home.

Volunteer to present it to club luncheons.

Call your mom at the office and read it to her.

Write it in a letter and mail it.

Put it on your dad's plate at supper.

Send it to a published writer.

Enter it in a contest.

Scribble it on your class DOODLE CLOTH
(a tablecloth kept just for important writing).

Take it to a college and share it with a class of
students who are preparing to be teachers.

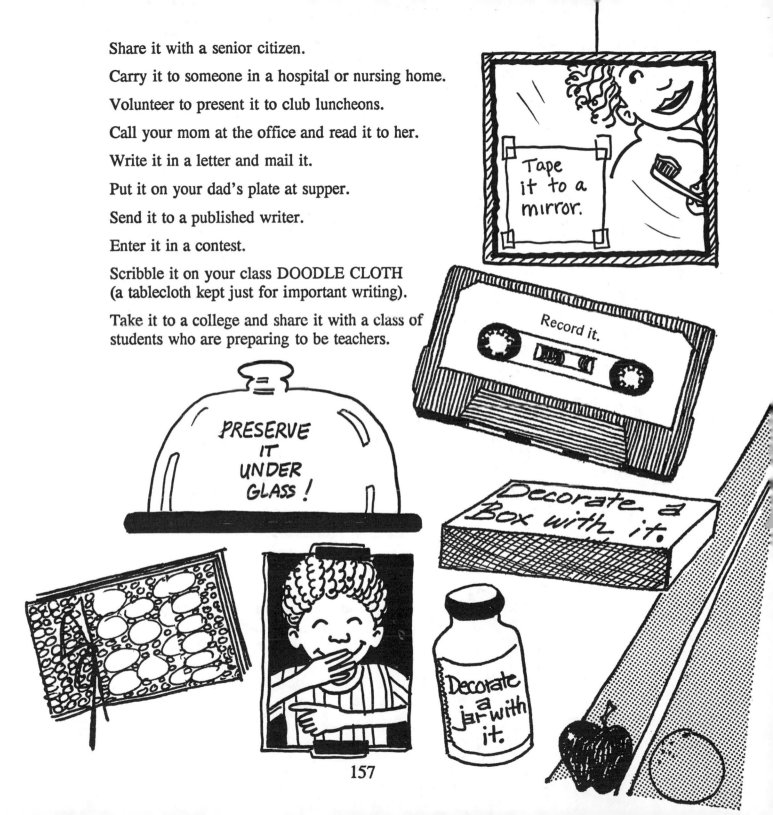

Tape it to a mirror.

Record it.

PRESERVE IT UNDER GLASS!

Decorate a Box with it.

Decorate a jar with it.

Put it on a flag

MAKE A MASK THAT FITS THE WRITING. WEAR THE MASK WHILE YOU SHARE IT.

Change it into a drama—and film it.

Paint it on wallpaper ...
>> or newspaper ...
>>> or bricks ...
>>>> or stones ...
>>>>> or old license plates ...

Publish it in a class newspaper ...
>> school paper ...
>>> PTA bulletin ...
>>>> community flier...

Hang it in store windows ...
>> church halls ...
>>> libraries ...
>>>> school buses ...

Show it off with a Poetry Party ...
>> a Poetry Parade...
>>> a Poetry Day...

Decorate the school's halls ...
>> walls ...
>>> doors ...
>>>> ceilings ...
>>>>> windows ...

Write it on posters ...
>> billboards ...
>>> blackboards ...

Keep personal collections in a diary ...
>> or a portfolio ...
>>> or a secret file ...

Hang it from window blinds ...
>> hangers ...
>>> a clothesline ...
>>>> doorframes ...

Write it up as a collection called *My Memoirs* and stash it away to read in ten years.

Memorize it and recite it to some friends.

Use it to start an "Add-Another-One" collection for the class writing center.

Join a writer's caucus so that you can enjoy and exchange with other writers.

Read it, accompanied by a gymnastic routine, as a halftime show at an athletic event.

Find (or produce) a piece of art to match the theme of your work.

Write it on a foggy or icy window.

Hang it from a tree (on biodegradable paper, please).

Try to publish it in your town newspaper.

Read it while someone creates sound effects or does a pantomime.

Create a shadow show to present while someone reads it.

Attach it to a helium balloon and set it free!

Transfer it to a wall-sized mural.

Send it to me. Really!

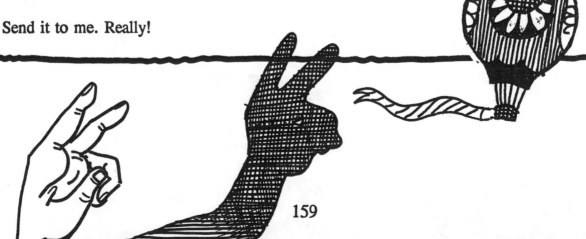

What I Learned From Doing My Portfolio

I learned to think about my writing.

I learned to get responses from other people.

I learned to do the writing process.

This helped me make my writing better.

My portfolio gives a picture of me as a writer.

---------- You'll be surprised at how my writing has changed this year. I write longer and better. My stuff shows my sense of humor. ----------

This is the portfolio of an awesome writer — me!

8

WRITING PORTFOLIOS

"What do portfolios have to do with teaching writing?"

A Natural Partnership
What Is A Writing Portfolio?
Purposes Of Writing Portfolios
Kinds Of Writing Portfolios
Inside The Portfolio
Don't Start Yet
Using Writing Portfolios

A NATURAL PARTNERSHIP

Portfolios are the best thing to happen to writing since *the discovery of process writing*. "Doing portfolios" is a process ... writing is a process ... and the two processes just blend together as nicely as hot fudge mixing in with melting ice cream. The two form a natural partnership that does wonders for writing instruction, writing improvement, and writing assessment. Here's why...

- Portfolios hold a rich resource of many kinds of writing on many topics—giving students a gold mine of samples for working on various stages of the writing process and various writing skills.

- Portfolios reveal **specific** struggles and successes writers are having with the process or with particular skills.

- Portfolios help kids see how **they** use the writing process.

- Portfolios unfold to teachers what is working, what is not working, and what is needed in their writing instruction.

- Portfolios become a moving, changing picture of a writer's growth—showing what writers have done and can do.

- Portfolios are a place where writers can showcase works that demonstrate various stages of the writing process.

- Portfolios help kids think about their writing ... and let them see themselves as real writers.

The material in this chapter is adapted from my recent book, Using WRITING PORTFOLIOS to Enhance Instruction and Assessment. This is a complete discussion of how and why to create writing portfolios and how to use them. It is published by Incentive Publications.

I hope you will include portfolios in your writing classroom. They don't have to be complex. They don't have to take gobs of time. You don't have to drop your current writing approach or system. You don't have to use portfolios for assessment. You can have any of dozens of different kinds, sizes, shapes—for any of dozens of purposes. But, however you do it, I think that once you add portfolios to your writing program, you'll find it's never quite the same again.

WHAT IS A WRITING PORTFOLIO?

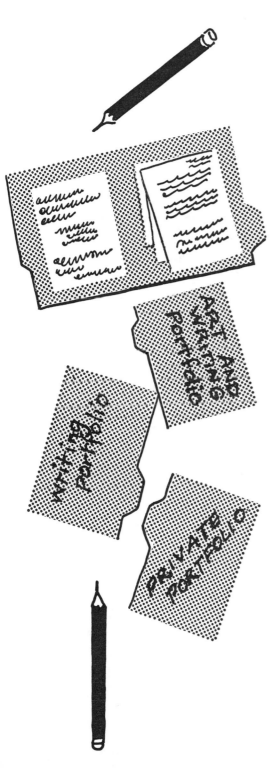

> *A writing portfolio is an organized and purposefully-selected collection of work that shows the student's writing achievement, efforts, growth, and attitudes.*

Ideally, this collection includes reasons for the selection of pieces, examples of student self-reflection on the work, and some evidence of student involvement in selecting, organizing, and reflecting. And **if the writing portfolio is going to be used for assessment (or evaluation) purposes ...** then it should also include criteria by which the pieces of writing (and/or the whole portfolio) will be judged.

Okay ... the above is **my** particular definition of a writing portfolio. No one can **exactly** prescribe for other teachers or writers the definition that fits best for them. However, I will put forth one of my biases here and suggest that there is an approach that best enhances the growth of writers. And, with this approach...

A writing portfolio is not...

... a random collection of writing.

... a folder of writing samples chosen and saved by the teacher.

... a collection of "special" writing created just **FOR** the portfolio

... just a collection of individual writing assignments to be looked at or considered separately from one another.

A writing portfolio is...

... writing samples chosen for a particular purpose.

... owned by the student and therefore shows much student participation in its creation and upkeep.

... a collection of work that shows growth.

... a whole picture of the student as a writer, learner, thinker.
   Each sample is seen as a part of the whole picture.

163

PURPOSES OF WRITING PORTFOLIOS

You've gotta have a purpose! All the decisions you make about your portfolios stem from the decision you make about the purpose. The kind of portfolio ... what goes in it ... how and why and how often things are selected ... what you do with it ... how it's shared ... all depend on why you're doing writing portfolios in the first place.

You may choose to use portfolios to increase the amount of writing kids do, or to broaden the number of genres they try, or to share writing with parents, or to give kids ownership of their writing. Writing portfolios can serve many different purposes. And no one reason is any more sacred or valuable than another.

The purposes of writing portfolios in each different setting should be decided by the teacher(s) and student(s) using the portfolio. The reason for this is that the purposes must be based on the needs of the particular writers, teacher, classroom, and writing program.

You know what your needs are. Start from there when you think about what purposes writing portfolios will serve in your classroom. They may serve one or many purposes. When you begin, settle on one or two—not a dozen. You can always add more later. Other needs will surface after you start working with the portfolios.

The sample purposes on the next page are but a few reasons some teachers choose to add portfolios to their writing classrooms.

164

SAMPLE PORTFOLIO PURPOSES

- to increase interest in writing
- to build excitement about writing
- to increase the amount of writing
- to increase variety in modes of writing
- to enjoy writing more
- to improve attitudes toward writing
- to develop greater confidence and self-esteem
- to introduce the writing process
- to improve use of the writing process
- to improve student writing
- to improve writing instruction
- to share writing with parents
- to measure writing growth
- to get students involved in evaluating their own writing
- to learn how students are working with the writing process
- to see how students think about the writing process
- to help students see themselves as writers
- to help students make choices about their writing
- to find out individuals' writing strengths and weaknesses
- to watch how writing improves over time
- to assess writing progress more accurately
- to see how writing instruction is working
- to teach students self-reflection skills
- to provide a record of writing growth from grades K-12

KINDS OF WRITING PORTFOLIOS

> **BIAS #20**
> **THERE IS NO ONE RIGHT OR BEST KIND OF WRITING PORTFOLIO**
>
> *There are many **right** kinds of portfolios for writing. What matters is that the portfolio's shape, size, complexity, structure, contents, and use be determined by the **purposes** of the portfolio.*

Writing portfolios come in all kinds, shapes, sizes. Some are very simple. Some are complex. Some span several months in time; others span years. They may contain many samples or few. They may be highly structured, or totally unstructured, or anywhere in between. Here are some of the possible kinds to consider:

The Working Portfolio—a storage folder for keeping many samples of writing and writing-related work gathered over time—the source from which pieces are selected for a permanent Writing Portfolio.

The Showcase Portfolio—a collection of writing selected to show off for any number of particular purposes.

The Process Portfolio—a collection of writing samples gathered to show the writing through the stages of the process.

The Pass-Along Portfolio—a collection of writing chosen specifically for the purpose of showing a writer's growth through several grades.

The Public Portfolio—a group of samples collected for sharing or viewing by others outside the classroom.

The Private Portfolio—a portfolio just for the owner's eyes.

The Project or Theme Portfolio—samples collected to show work, thinking, or growth on a topic or area of study, or on one theme.

The Group Portfolio—samples gathered by a group or whole class and put together for a specific purpose.

The Teacher's Portfolio—highly recommended! The teacher should keep a writing portfolio of the same kind as students keep.

INSIDE THE PORTFOLIO

To have a writing portfolio, you've got to have a bunch of writing! So have students keep writing of all kinds ... in all stages ... on many topics. This will be the storehouse from which they can select pieces to move into their writing portfolios. And when that happens, their portfolios might include such things as...

- works in progress
- finished works
- responses to literature
- journal entries
- home writing projects
- writing interest inventory
- display of favorite words
- photo essay
- mini-books
- piece written for a specific audience
- audio tape of an original written work
- writing from other subject areas
- early piece/later piece
- pieces from various times of the year
- favorite or fun piece
- important piece
- satisfying piece (or unsatisfying piece)
- best piece (or worst piece)
- piece that gave me trouble
- most exciting piece
- piece I'd like to throw away
- free pick, teacher pick, parent pick
- peer, parent, teacher reflections
- pieces scored with a scoring guide
- comparisons of two pieces
- self-reflections on pieces

MORE WRITING PORTFOLIO CONTENTS...

- samples of different kinds of writing

- pre-writing examples ... webs, outlines, clusters, collections of phrases, words, charts, ideas, etc.

- Process Package—samples which show a piece of writing through all the stages of the writing process

- Biography of a Work—a written explanation, chart, or diagram, detailing how the writer went about creating the work

- works that show writer's work on various writing traits—such as word choice, organization, ideas and content, clarity, voice, sentence fluency, conventions

- work that reflects various modes of writing such as descriptive, imaginative, persuasive, expository, narrative

- illustrations, graphics, or photos created to accompany writing

- writing within artwork (ads, cartoons, posters, storyboards,etc.)

- items, notes, ideas, pictures, and other examples of something that sparked writing

It's good for portfolios to include...
- A list of contents
- A letter of introduction or purpose
- Multiple samples
- A variety of kinds of writing
- Samples collected over time
- Dates on all entries
- Samples that show growth
- Reasons for each selection
- Student self-reflections

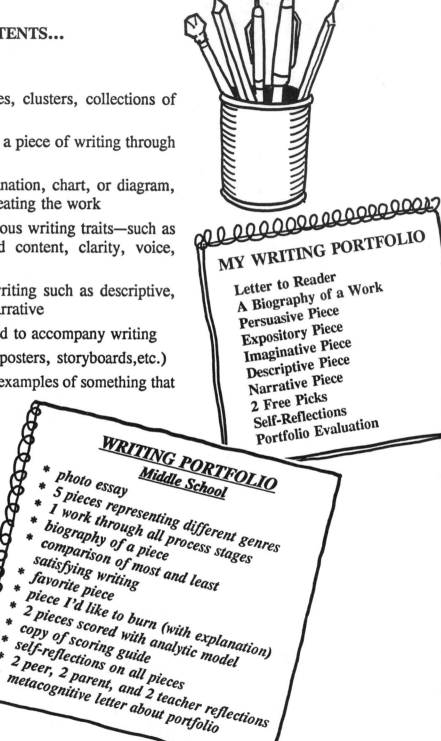

MY WRITING PORTFOLIO

Letter to Reader
A Biography of a Work
Persuasive Piece
Expository Piece
Imaginative Piece
Descriptive Piece
Narrative Piece
2 Free Picks
Self-Reflections
Portfolio Evaluation

WRITING PORTFOLIO
Middle School

* photo essay
* 5 pieces representing different genres
* 1 work through all process stages
* biography of a piece
* comparison of most and least satisfying writing
* favorite piece
* piece I'd like to burn (with explanation)
* 2 pieces scored with analytic model
* copy of scoring guide
* self-reflections on all pieces
* 2 peer, 2 parent, and 2 teacher reflections
* metacognitive letter about portfolio

WRITING PORTFOLIO
grade 1

Letter about my Portfolio (dictated)
Photo Essay (pictures and sentences of *Things I Can Do*)
Collage of words and phrases that I can read (cut from magazines)
The Lost Tooth—My Favorite Writing
Computer print-out of words I can type
My favorite poem, *No Flu at the Zoo*
Me, picture of me with describing words
Sentences from Home
Audio Tapes of self-reflections

MEGAN'S WRITING PORTFOLIO

Megan DiGiarnno, Grade 4, Avon School

Letter to My Readers

Collection of good ideas for future writing

Idea Web for "Rapunzel" news article

Best Work from Fall

Best Work from Winter

Piece through all stages

Piece I Had A Tough Time Writing

Most Fun Piece

Self-Reflections (attached to each piece)

Peer Reflection

Mid-Year Portfolio Evaluation Letter

5th Grade WRITING, ART, MUSIC PORTFOLIO

* letter explaining purpose of portfolio
* 3 writing samples: most important, most improved, and most fun
* writing "Process Package"
* biography of an art creation
* 3 art samples: toughest, favorite, and needs changing
* video performance of original song, "I Left My Heart in Peoria"
* slides of art mural and wire sculpture
* most unusual computer graphics
* written personal theme song
* original poem with art piece and music melody to match
* audio tape of percussion rhythm I created for electronic keyboard
* reflections from self and others
* letter explaining how my portfolio shows the connections between art, music, and writing

MY WRITING PORTFOLIO

Portfolio Introduction Letter
My Best Work
Comparison of An Early & A Later Piece
An Illustrated Piece
Most Important Piece
Hardest Piece
Self-Reflections
Peer Reflection
Parent Reflection

DON'T START YET

Portfolios are such a good idea that, if you're not doing them already, you may be tempted to jump right into them here and now. **Resist the temptation!** It's important ... no, it's absolutely essential ... that you do some planning first. So before you get started, think about...

The fit with your writing program—Do you need portfolios? ... How will portfolio use fit into your current instruction? ... What will need to be changed, rearranged, dropped, added, adapted?

Your readiness—Portfolio use often challenges usual assumptions and changes roles. Will the portfolio process succeed in your current classroom conditions? ... Are your students ready? ... Are you?

Planning—Who will take part in the planning for your writing portfolio process? ... When will planning begin? ... How and where?

Your goals—What will be the purposes of writing portfolios in your classroom? ... What do you want students to be able to do or know?

Who, what, and when—Which classes will create portfolios? ... What kind of portfolios will they be? ... When will you begin?

The outsides and insides—What containers? ... How will they look? ... What will go inside?

Management—Who will own the writing portfolios? ... Who will have access? ... How will they be handled and stored? ... How will selections be made? ... How often? ... By whom? ... How will portfolios be reviewed? ... What kinds of records will be kept? ... What will happen to them at the end of the year? ... etc.

Assessment—Will the writing portfolios be used for assessment? ... How? ... By whom? ... With what criteria? ... What will you do with assessment results?

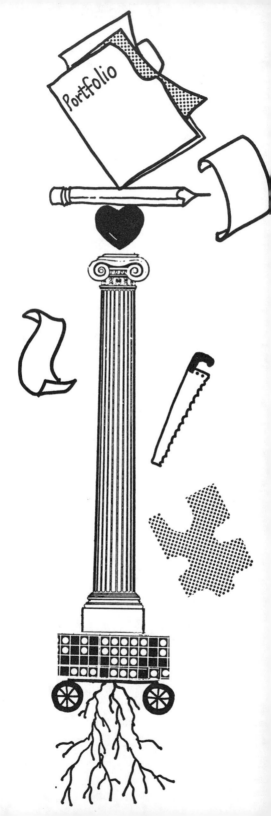

170

PORTFOLIO ADVICE

- PLAN. THINK ... before you start.

- Do your homework. Learn all you can about portfolios. There are many excellent books, workshops, video tapes, and other resources out there to help you.

- Make sure your kids are doing plenty of writing assignments that are relevant. This way they'll have important, meaningful writing available for working into portfolios.

- Start small and keep it simple. A complex system will drive you crazy and overwhelm your students.

- Train students to reflect on writing and writing portfolios. Do lots of casual reflecting before you even begin to make portfolio collections.

- Take your time. "Grow" into portfolio use gradually over the year. You don't have to do it all at once.

- Keep your own portfolio. This is the best way to learn about the portfolio process—firsthand.

- Talk to other teachers. Share ideas, struggles, discoveries.

- Don't try to replace your other good writing instruction. Writing portfolios can fit into your present program.

- Keep parents informed and involved all along the way.

- LISTEN to your students. They will tell you what's working and what isn't.

USING PORTFOLIOS

No two systems for doing writing portfolios will be the same, since no two classrooms are identical. The following steps are a suggestion of a way to help you form your own plan for getting started...

1. **Write ... write ... write.** The portfolio process really begins with and centers around students' writing.

2. **Introduce the portfolio concept to students.** The best way to do this is to bring some portfolios into the classroom (your own ... some from other classes ... an artist's ... a writer's ... a photographer's). Talk about the contents, purposes, appearance.

3. **Agree on the purposes for your writing portfolios.** Discuss these with students and anyone else involved in planning.

4. **Make working portfolios and begin collecting writing ...** all sizes, shapes, kinds, stages, lengths, purposes, topics, subjects.

5. **Communicate with parents.** Through a letter, a class visit, a newspaper, an announcement ... let parents in on what you'll be doing and why. Tell them what to expect from portfolios.

6. **Train students to reflect on writing.** They need plenty of practice responding to writing of all kinds. They need to **learn** what to look for, how to make helpful comments, and how to make use of feedback. Don't short-cut this task. Responding to writing is a key skill in the process of using writing portfolios.

7. **Design and create permanent portfolios.** Dedicate enough time for students to design, create, and decorate the permanent writing portfolio. The outside "container" tells a lot about the portfolio owner, and is an important part of the total portfolio.

8. **Make management decisions.** Students and teacher must be clear on management issues ... portfolio storage ... portfolio access ... how and when and how often and by whom selections will be made ... portfolio organization ... time to work on them ... conferences ... portfolio review and/or evaluation ... etc.

9. **Have students select samples.** Once the containers are ready, students can select samples according to agreed-upon selection guidelines. Make sure they know what and when to select. It's also important to have students label each piece selected with a comment or description that tells why the piece was chosen.

10. **Ask students to reflect on pieces.** When the student selects a sample for the portfolio, it's a good time to do some sort of reflection. This may be just a phrase or sentence about why the piece was chosen or it may be a detailed analysis of the writer's process, strengths, or reactions. There are many possible ways for kids of all ages to reflect. This may be done orally by young writers. Writers may request reflections from others at this time... peers, parents, teachers, friends, neighbors...

11. **Organize portfolios.** This may include attaching reflections, sequencing items, making a Table of Contents, etc. It is especially important for kids to do this before the portfolio is viewed by someone else, before a conference, or before the portfolio is to be evaluated. Give them time to do this.

12. **Gather reflections.** After it's organized, the owner may present the portfolio for teacher review and/or scoring. He/ she may also solicit peer or parent reflections on the portfolio.

13. **Review student portfolios yourself.** Keep notes on what students' portfolios tell you about individuals' progress and needs and about writing in your classroom. **Then make use of what you learn.** Find out some things about what is working and what is needed. Use the information you gain from portfolios to make changes in instruction.

THE SOLDIER

A poem written suddenly
    Outpouring onto paper
Scribbled down hurriedly
    While thoughts are hot still
Becomes a soldier, defiant, free,
    To fight my war, to fight for me.

An onslaught of words, defending me,
    Goes forth like a brave trooper
From his home. And now,
    Without author, stands alone.

But it returns, beaten, red marks like wounds
Slashing the innocent lines,
    The struggle over.
The wounds are deep. They reach
    To scar my soul which cries out:
"Understand!" The feeling, not the grammar,
    Should be read! Now the soldier is dead.
The poem that he was lies crumpled
    In a corner, the effort made in vain.

The enemy has won.

by Rencie Farwell
Grade 6

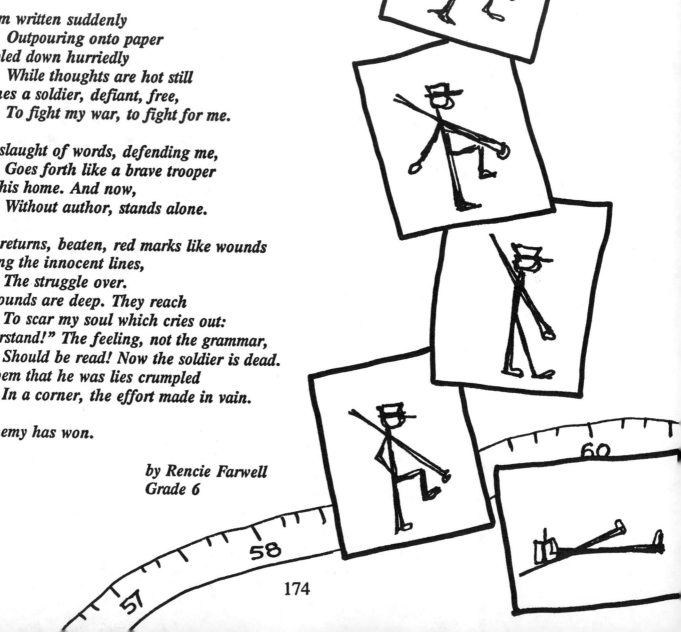

174

9

ASSESSMENT

"I'm not sure how to evaluate writing!"

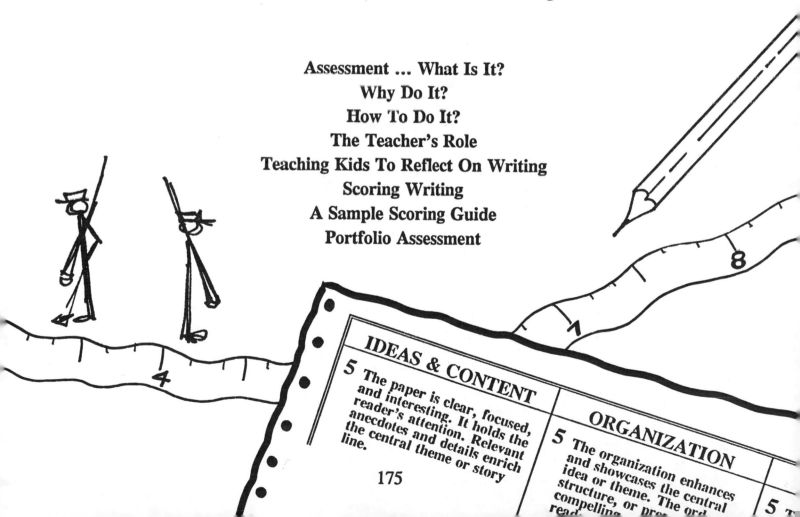

IDEAS & CONTENT

5 The paper is clear, focused, and interesting. It holds the reader's attention. Relevant anecdotes and details enrich the central theme or story line.

175

ORGANIZATION

5 The organization enhances and showcases the central idea or theme. The ord structure, or pre compelling read

ASSESSMENT ... WHAT IS IT?

ASSESS: *to evaluate or appraise*

EVALUATE: *to determine the worth of; to examine and judge*

Now this is a tough one—assigning value to a piece of writing! These words are loaded with the implication that we're judging quality ... value ... and worth. And that's serious stuff. It's particularly serious because judgments of a person's *writing* come pretty close to judgments of the *writer*—which is something to embark on with great care ... and with great humility. If you didn't stop to read the poem on page 174 when you began this chapter, go back now and listen to a 6th grader's view of what evaluation means to a writer.

Before we teachers start on programs which lead to the evaluation of writing and writers, let's think carefully about what we're doing, how we're doing it, why we're doing it, and—most seriously—how it affects the writers. Then maybe we'll have a good chance of appraising writing in ways that do not make writers feel as if they're being attacked (and possibly defeated) by an enemy.

> ### BIAS #21
> ### IT'S NOT SOMETHING TO DO AT THE END
> *Evaluation should (and does) happen throughout the writing process and is definitely not something to save for doing to the final product.*

This is a good place to start thinking about what assessment is. Traditionally, assessment has meant ... trying to find out what a writer can do by looking at (and somehow grading) the writing after the writer feels it is finished or polished. This approach ignores evaluative steps that **are** going on in other parts of the process. It also misses out on the wonderful opportunities for learning and growth that come from integrating assessment into the whole writing process and from involving the writers in assessing their own work.

KIDS are using evaluation processes whenever they...

... decide which collected ideas to use (or drop) in their rough draft.

... reflect on their own writing.

... give responses to work written by peers or other writers.

... listen to what others say about their writing.

... decide what responses from others to use in their revisions.

... look at their own rough draft and make revisions.

... compare one piece of their writing to another piece.

... use a scoring guide to assess their own (or others') writing.

... choose to leave something out, add something, change something, correct something during revision.

... check for and change mechanics.

... decide to present (or not present) a piece of writing.

... make selections for their portfolios.

... reflect on portfolio selections.

... reflect on the entire portfolio.

... prepare for writing or portfolio conferences.

... discuss their writing at a conference.

... participate in any one of writing process stages 2-7.

YOU, the TEACHER, are evaluating when you...

... watch them write ... giving responses, help, and encouragement.

... write with them ... making comments and suggestions.

... give responses (orally or in writing) to students' writing.

... teach lessons on response and revision.

... model response and revision of your own or others' writing.

... assist them with ANY stage of the writing process.

... review their writing at ANY stage of the process.

... keep anecdotal notes as you watch them work.

... review their writing in preparation for conferences.

... discuss writing with a writer at a conference.

... keep notes or other records from a conference.

... score their writing with a scoring guide.

... prepare grades for the report card.

... prepare for and conduct parent-teacher conferences.

... review portfolios and/or respond to portfolios.

... score or otherwise evaluate portfolios.

WHY DO IT?

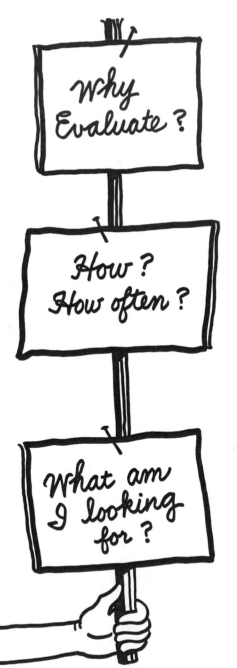

> **BIAS #22**
> **ASSESSMENT IS ABOUT GROWTH**
> *Unless the goal is growth for writers, assessment only labels where they are now...and does little to help them go anywhere else with their writing.*

When you make plans or take steps to assess or grade or examine kids' writing, start by asking yourself...

What does evaluation mean to me?

Why evaluate? How? How often?

What am I looking for?

What do I want students to know or be able to do?

How will I be able to tell when they can (or can't) do it?

By what criteria are the writers or the writing judged?

Do the writers know what the criteria are?

What will I do with the evaluative information when I get it?

All these questions have to do with WHY you evaluate writing. You might do it because...

... you **have** to give grades for writing on the report cards.

... you need to tell parents what their kids can do.

... you want to find out what students have accomplished in writing.

... your school wants to collect data on students' abilities in writing.

... you want to find out if your writing instruction is working.

... you want to know writers' strengths and needs so you can modify your instruction and plan experiences to help writers improve.

... you want the writers to be able to see their own strengths, needs, growth, abilities, and progress.

I always argue for assessment that is rooted in and intricately connected to the writing process. Not all assessment is. And so not all assessment contributes to growth of writers and writing.

The reasons for evaluation must have to do with writers (and their teachers) finding out what they can do, what they cannot do, what they can sort-of do, what is working, what is not working, what's been tried, what hasn't ... **all for the purpose of building writers, improving writing, and improving writing instruction.**

I urge you to examine your own assessment purposes and priorities to see if **the writers** and their growth ... in using ALL parts of the writing process for many kinds and purposes of writing ... **is the top priority.** Other priorities are okay, too, but this should be first.

I also urge you to consider what role your students play in writing assessment in your classroom. Often, students head into writing assignments **not** really knowing what is expected. Nor do they know if or when or by what criteria the writing will be judged. So they write. Then they sit helplessly by as their writing is scrutinized and scored, examined and evaluated. They can only wait for a verdict ... from someone else ... to tell them how they're doing.

Assessment is **not** the private property of teachers. Kids **can** learn to evaluate their own writing. They must take part in this ... it is central to the growth of writing. Even before they write, they need to know about what makes writing strong or effective. **And they need to know the criteria by which their own writing will be judged.** They cannot aim for a good performance if they don't know what constitutes a good performance.

BIAS #23
**THE REAL PURPOSE OF EVALUATION
IS FOR KIDS TO LEARN
TO EVALUATE THEMSELVES**

What's most important in the whole process of evaluation is for kids to gain tools they can use to make decisions and judgments that will help them value and improve their own writing.

179

HOW TO DO IT?

"Authentic" writing assessment is one of the most exciting developments in the field of writing these days. With years of using the writing process under our belts, educators are now learning how to really find out what writers can do and what they need. I've been in many classrooms where assessment is closely connected to the writing process and writing instruction ... where it is truly helping writers grow ... and where kids are as deeply involved in it as teachers. The assessment plan in these classrooms usually involves a combination of many of these elements:

... kids reflecting on writing—their own and others

... kids giving responses to one another's writing in pairs, small groups, and/or large groups (orally and/or in writing)

... teachers giving responses to kids' writing

... kids giving responses to teachers' writing

... kids asking for responses from teachers, parents, peers, friends

... teachers helping writers expand evaluating and responding skills

... teachers suggesting new ways to examine and think about writing

... teachers casually visiting with writers and keeping anecdotal notes about strengths, needs, problems, accomplishments

... kids evaluating pieces with a writing rubric or scoring guide

... teachers and kids using a scoring guide together

... kids making writing portfolio selections

... kids reviewing their writing in preparation for conferences

... teachers conferencing with kids about individual pieces of writing, several pieces of writing, or portfolios

... teachers keeping records of student writing, growth, progress, needs, problems over a period of time

... teachers evaluating their writing instruction based on a review of student needs and progress

Celebrate strengths.

Model reflection skills.

Teach reflection skills.

reflections of a writer

Keep good records.

Evaluate DURING the process

Give kids SPECIFIC feedback.

Avoid false praise.

180

LOOK FOR GROWTH IN...

- **comfort with writing**
- **willingness to write**
- **willingness and ability to think about his/her writing**
- **thinking of herself/himself as a writer**
- **use of the writing process**
- **understanding of the stages of the process**
- **the use of writing skills or traits**
  (See skills on pages 126-127 and traits on pages 188-189.)
- **willingness to respond to and revise writing**
- **participation and effectiveness in responses to writing**
- **comfort and ability with revision**
- **complexity of writing and revision tasks she/he can handle**
- **ability to compare pieces of writing**
- **comfort and facility with increased number of genres and styles**
- **ability to reflect on writing**
- **complexity of evaluation processes**
- **ability to see progress, growth, and needs in his/her own writing**
- **willingness and ability to talk about her/his writing**

These are some of the kinds of skills, behaviors, and changes to assess when writers and writing are evaluated. They cannot all be assessed with any one assessment tool. Use a variety of approaches (see page 180) that get at many different aspects of writing growth. Start with what writers are doing **now** and watch where they go, how they change, what they learn. And, always, keep **the writers' growth** as the primary reason for doing assessment at all.

Remember ... in putting forth personal writing, a child is sending forth his or her self "like a brave trooper." The student should be **sure**, before beginning to write ... and, especially, before sharing the finished product ... that you, the teacher, are an **ally**—not an enemy.

Use Of Writing Skills
Portfolio Use
Self-reflection
Word Choice
Use of the Writing Process
Organization
Ideas
Voice

Wow! I've grown!

THE TEACHER'S ROLE

I've said that assessment is about growth. We want our kids to grow as writers. We want to examine their writing and evaluate their performances to increase the *quality* of their writing. So how do young writers acquire or improve *quality*?

I have a taste for writing.

> ## BIAS #24
> ## EXPOSURE BUILDS TASTE AND QUALITY
>
> *The constant reading and sharing of writing—with consistent attention drawn to effective tools and good techniques—brings students gradually to a sense of what constitutes good writing.*

When kids come into contact with many examples of interesting, powerful writing ... when they write, respond to writing, and revise their own and others' writing again and again ... they begin to absorb the concepts of what works well, what captures the reader, what sounds pleasing, what makes sense. And with time, **they begin to submit to those concepts.** The good stuff rubs off on them, and sneaks its way into their own writing.

A teacher **can't give** a child a sense of taste or an eye for what's good. You **can,** however, help someone acquire it by...

... exposing him—a lot—to a variety of good writing.
... drawing attention to effective, interesting, powerful, or pleasing ways with words and language.
... giving her plenty of practice responding to writing.
... giving him models for reflecting on his own writing.
... providing directions for writing that challenge and excite.
... being close by while she's trying the process.
... supporting and building his attempts as a writer.

182

I have to stop and confess right here that I don't believe I, as a teacher, can or should examine a piece of finished writing from a student and evaluate it in the strictest sense of that word ... to "determine worth." How can I say, *"This idea is not valuable,"* or *"This thought is worthwhile"*?

> ## BIAS #25
> ## THE TEACHER IS NOT THE FINAL CRITIC
> *It is the teacher's job to help the writer during the writing process ... to help him/her develop the best work possible ... to give aid while the writing is in unfinished form—NOT to judge the final product.*

As I've insisted earlier, evaluation is going on throughout all the stages of the process. And the teacher is a model, catalyst, and helper in that evaluation each step of the way. It is **too late**—and of little help—for the teacher to say of the final piece, *weak* or *strong*. If a piece is *weak*, why didn't I help the kid make it stronger while she was working on it? How dare I declare it *weak* at this stage?

This doesn't mean that the teacher gives no response to final products. Response given to polished pieces will certainly help the writer with the next piece, and will strengthen understandings about effective writing in general. But it doesn't strengthen the finished piece. The piano teacher or dance instructor's job isn't to judge the artist's performance at the recital. That job is for the judges or the critics. The instructor's guidance is needed by the pianist or dancer while he or she is **learning** ... in the hours and weeks and years **before** the big performance. It is **much more valuable** for the teacher to give input **during** the process than at the end.

Who is, then, the final critic of writers? I believe there are two: THE STUDENT—fulfillment and comfort with her/his own work, and LIFE—the current and eventual effectiveness of the person's written expression and communication.

183

TEACHING KIDS TO REFLECT ON WRITING

One of the most important components of writing assessment is the student's evaluation of her or his own writing. This is frequently called self-reflection, because the writer takes time to stop and reflect on a piece of writing and/or on herself or himself as a writer. In addition to self-reflection, writers can gather reflections or responses from others ... such as peers, parents, and teachers.

Reflection can be done in many ways, from simple to complex. It can be written or oral. It can address many different aspects of writing—not necessarily all at once. As you teach your students to reflect, you'll need to select approaches that fit their ages and needs.

You will find that as kids gain experience with reflecting, they move from simple, straightforward observations (such as comments on the writing's neatness, length, or conventions) to more complex reflections (such as comparisons between pieces, explanations of the processes she used, or analysis of himself as a writer).

WAYS TO DO IT

open-ended sentences to finish
questions for writers to answer
brief comments on sticky notes
short sentences
letters to the author
letters to the reader
reflection forms to complete
reflection checklists
evauative essays or paragraphs

THINGS TO FOCUS ON...
(listed from simple to complex)

appearance of the writing
conventions
word choice and use
ideas and content
writing techniques and genres
processes the writer uses
comparisons between uses
growth and change in writing
portfolio analysis

TYPES OF REFLECTIONS

what you think of a piece
what you liked about a piece
strengths & weaknesses of a piece
what a piece accomplishes
purpose of a piece
what a piece shows about the writer
comparisons of 2 or more works
analysis of the writer's process
why a piece was selected for a portfolio
analysis of a whole portfolio

To help students learn and grow in reflection skills...

- Model reflective responses and comments in the classroom.
- Reflect on learning and performances in all subject areas.
- Practice orally reflecting on writing ... often.
- Start simple. Encourage short comments, sentences to finish, reflections on just **one** thing.
- Give kids a variety of ways to reflect. Don't get stuck on one tactic, such as, *"This was good because..."* Try different statements such as:

    *What I like best about this (or what I **don't** like) is...*
    I wish I could change...
    The hardest part of the process was...
    This was fun to write because...
    I struggled with...
    My favorite part of this is...

    and ask questions such as:

    What did you do well in this piece?
    What problems did you have with the writing?
    How does this compare with the last piece?
    Why are you satisfied (or unsatisfied) with this?
    What is your biggest strength as a writer?
    How did you go about writing this piece?
    What does this piece show about you as a writer?
    How has your writing changed?

- Be aware that many forms and checklists may limit student reflections. Open-ended reflections and reflection forms that kids create work best.
- Help kids think about themselves as writers.
- Writing doesn't have to be polished to reflect on it. Reflect at various stages of the process.
- Don't be surprised if kids find it hard to say positive things about their writing. They'll need practice in celebrating growth!
- Remember that kids grow at different rates in their ability to reflect. Celebrate their reflection—simple or complex.

SCORING WRITING

Sometimes a *scoring guide* (or *rubric*) is used to analyze pieces of writing. This is a more "formal" way to assess writing performance than some other evaluative measures because it examines a specific set of writing skills against clear criteria and yields a numerical score.

This way of evaluating writing is **not** necessarily better than other assessment techniques. Self-reflections, reflections from others, writing conferences, interviews with the teacher, responses from editing partners—all these give important evaluative information to teachers and writers. But this method is fitting for certain assessment needs. It yields some information that is not easy to get in other ways. A scoring guide can be an excellent addition to the total package of tools for assessment of writing performance and growth.

Here are some of the benefits of using a good scoring guide to evaluate a piece of writing:

- The guide identifies specific writing traits (characteristics) that are important to know about, practice, and try to improve.

- The guide includes clear criteria for what constitutes a good performance in each of the traits identified.

- Because the writing traits are identified, and the criteria are spelled out ... **students know what the standards are.** They know what to aim for in working on writing.

- Teachers also know what to aim for and look for. They have a consistent standard by which to consider student performance—no more guessing about what's good.

- The scoring guide is a wonderful instructional tool. It can be used not only to rate a piece of writing, but also to serve as a model of what to work toward for improved writing in each of the areas that the guide identifies.

VAGUE WORDS . 3 . ORDINARY LANGUAGE   BETTER SELECTIONS . . 5 . FULL, RICH WORD

My ideas really measure up!

Scoring guides must be used thoughtfully, however. As with any other evaluative tool, writers and teachers must know what the purpose is, why and how it is to be used, what to do with the information gained, and how it benefits writers. And they must know what can't be learned from it. I always advise...

- **Don't score every piece of writing.** This will discourage writers and probably kill writing. It's not necessary. Score a piece now and then, particularly when the writer wants to learn how she/he is handling a particular trait. The scoring of writing samples should be **only one** part of a plan for writing assessment in the classroom. Be aware that **only some** of the growth can be measured by a scoring guide. If it's all you use for assessment, you won't be getting the whole picture of a writer's work and development.

- **You don't need to use the whole rubric.** Most scoring guides are complex and weighty, with several traits identified. Think about "slicing" the guide into strips so students can work on one trait at a time. Later on, you may get to the point where the teacher or writer wants to score a piece in all the trait areas.

- **Beware of focusing on final products only.** If you use the scoring guide only to analyze finished products, you've missed out on many possibilities for learning and growth. The performance goals on a scoring guide **are a great help** to writers while they are **in** the process—particularly during the responding-revision stages.

- **Share it with students.** The scoring guide is not just the property of the teacher. Students of all ages can learn to use these, especially if they are rewritten in student-friendly language. Give students lots of opportunities to score their own writing, anonymous writing, or writing done by classmates (or by the teacher).

> *The sample scoring guide on pages 188-189 is used in my home state, Oregon, for direct writing assessment throughout the state. I share this with you because I find it to be clear, thorough, and very useful for writing assessment and instruction. It is used with permission of the Oregon Department of Education, 255 Capitol Street NE, Salem, Oregon 97310.*

THE OREGON DIRECT WRITING ASSESSMENT...

IDEAS & CONTENT	ORGANIZATION	VOICE
5 The paper is clear, focused, and interesting. It holds the reader's attention. Relevant anecdotes and details enrich the central theme or story line.	**5** The organization enhances and showcases the central idea or theme. The order, structure, or presentation is compelling and moves the reader through the text.	**5** The writer speaks directly to the reader in a way that is individualistic, expressive, and engaging. Clearly, the writer is involved in the text and is writing to be read.
3 The paper is clear and focused, even though the overall result may not be captivating. Support is attempted, but it may be limited, insubstantial, too general, or out of balance with the main ideas.	**3** The reader can readily follow what's being said, but the overall organization may sometimes be ineffective or too obvious.	**3** The writer seems sincere but not fully involved in the topic. The result is pleasant, acceptable, sometimes even personable, but not compelling.
1 The paper lacks a central idea or purpose, or forces the reader to make inferences based on very sketchy details.	**1** Organization is haphazard and disjointed. The writing lacks direction, with ideas, details, or events strung together helter-skelter.	**1** The writer seems wholly indifferent, uninvolved, or dispassionate. As a result, the writing is flat, lifeless, stiff, or mechanical. It may even be (depending on the topic) overly technical or jargonistic.

Due to the length of the scoring guide, I have included it in an abbreviated form. What is missing from each section is a list of further details under each category. These elaborations on the description for each number give more specifics to the person doing the scoring. A score of 1-5 may be given for each trait. Although the scores of 2 and 4 are not described, the scorer may believe a paper deserves an in-between score in a certain trait.

...ANALYTIC TRAIT SCORING GUIDE

WORD CHOICE	SENTENCE FLUENCY	CONVENTIONS
5 Words convey the intended message in an interesting, precise, and natural way. The writing is full and rich, yet concise.	**5** The writing has an easy flow and rhythm when read aloud. Sentences are well built, with consistently strong and varied structure that makes expressive oral reading easy and enjoyable.	**5** The writer demonstrates a good grasp of standard writing conventions (such as grammar, capitalization, punctuation, usage, spelling, paragraphing) and uses them effectively to enhance readability. Errors tend to be so few and so minor that the reader can easily skim right over them unless specifically searching for them.
3 The language is quite ordinary, but it does convey the message. It's functional, even if it lacks punch. Often, the writer settles for what's easy or handy, producing a sort of "generic paper" stuffed with familiar words and phrases.	**3** Sentences tend to be mechanical rather than fluid. The text hums along efficiently for the most part, though it may lack a certain rhythm or grace, tending to be more pleasant than musical. Occasional awkward constructions force the reader to slow down or reread.	**3** Errors in writing conventions, while not overwhelming, begin to impair readability. While errors do not block meaning, they tend to be distracting.
1 The writer struggles with a limited vocabulary, groping for words to convey meaning. Often the language is so vague or abstract or so redundant and devoid of detail that only the broadest, most general sort of message comes through.	**1** The paper is difficult to follow or to read aloud. Sentences tend to be choppy, incomplete, rambling, irregular, or just very awkward.	**1** Numerous errors in usage, sentence structure, spelling, or punctuation repeatedly distract the reader and make the text difficult to read. In fact, the severity and the frequency of errors tend to be so overwhelming that the reader finds it very difficult to focus on the message and must reread for meaning.

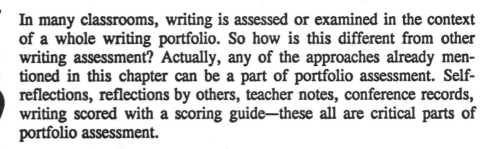

PORTFOLIO REFLECTIONS

Why did I select this piece for my portfolio?

What does this portfolio show about me as a writer?

What did I learn from doing my portfolio?

What do I want a reader to know about this portfolio?

What changes does the portfolio show in my writing?

What have I learned from doing a writing portfolio?

What is the best thing about keeping a writing portfolio?

PORTFOLIO ASSESSMENT

In many classrooms, writing is assessed or examined in the context of a whole writing portfolio. So how is this different from other writing assessment? Actually, any of the approaches already mentioned in this chapter can be a part of portfolio assessment. Self-reflections, reflections by others, teacher notes, conference records, writing scored with a scoring guide—these all are critical parts of portfolio assessment.

What is different about portfolio assessment is this ... each piece of writing is seen as **a part of a body of work** that tells about the writer. Even if a piece is evaluated, reflected upon, or scored separately, it is also viewed as a part of a whole picture.

So portfolio assessment requires that writers and teachers focus on...
... the writer's growth and change over a period of time.
... the pieces of writing in relation to the whole collection.
... the processes involved in selecting, organizing, and evaluating the writing within the portfolio.
... the processes of reflecting on the portfolio as a whole.

This means that teachers and writers must ask all the same questions about assessment that you saw on page 178. But, in addition, they consider how the entire body of work will be examined and scored or otherwise evaluated.

If you are going to use writing portfolios for the purpose of assessing writing, I recommend that you prepare criteria by which the portfolio will be judged. This can be in the form of a scoring guide or list of expectations, portfolio review checklist, conference record, or evaluation chart. (See sample Writing Portfolio Scoring Guide on page 191.) The best forms for portfolio assessment are the ones you and your students design to suit your own needs.

what do you think of yourself as writer?

WRITING PORTFOLIO
Scoring Guide

	1 Needs Much Improvement	2 Adequate	3 Strong
Variety and Quantity of Writing	limited quantity, little or no variety of forms, not a broad collection	acceptable number, variety and versatility of writing forms and purposes	rich variety of kinds of writing showing versatility of writing attempts and ability
Writing Skills and Traits	limited demonstration of various writing techniques, weak development of traits	evidence of experience with several traits, attention to text and surface features, ideas are developed	good control of several writing skills and traits, ideas and organization lead to clear, understandable writing
Writing Process	shows little or no grasp of writing strategies and processes	uses the writing process, can describe how he/she approaches writing	obvious facility with all phases of the writing process, samples of stages are evident in portfolio
Evidence of Growth	little change seen from early to late pieces, little sense of self as writer, little engagement with writing, poor at setting personal goals	some growth seen from early to later pieces, some sense of self as writer, evidence of goal setting	progress evident, increased use of writing processes and skills, identifies self as writer, sets personal standards and goals
Self–Evaluation	no reflections or narrow, one-dimensional evaluations	expanding self-evaluations, able to identify characteristics of own writing	clear, specific reflections increasing in variety and depth
Portfolio Processes	poor presentation and organization, has difficulty with preparing and caretaking portfolio	shows organization, ownership, interest, increased independence in managing own portfolio	takes responsibility, independence in managing portfolio, good appearance and organization
Personal Involvement and Attitude	little or no attachment to portfolio or sense of accomplishment or pride	takes pride in ownership, takes some initiative and control of portfolio, feels sense of worth	takes great pride in ownership, enthusiastic, enjoys taking responsibility for learning

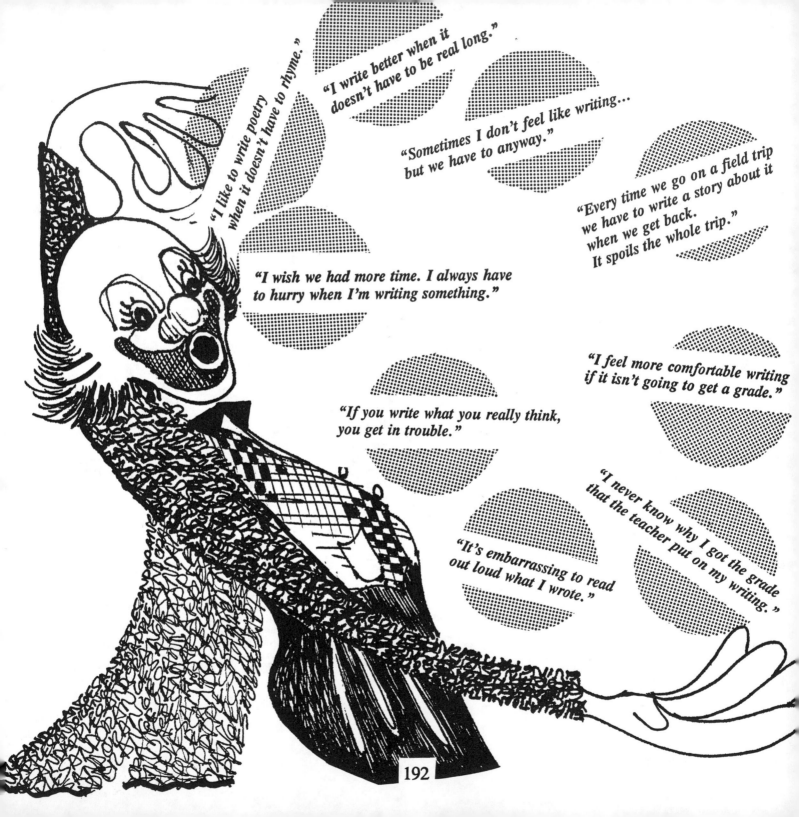

"It's easier for me when the teacher reads some examples first."

"I like when we write about ourselves."

"My favorite part is listening to each other's writing."

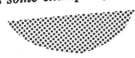

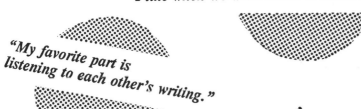

"When the teacher just says, 'Write a poem...' I can't think of anything."

"I hate getting my paper back all marked up."

"I like to write when we're allowed to write about anything we want."

"It's better to write in class instead of for homework."

"I like getting help with mistakes."

10

PROBLEMS

"I have this kid who just WON'T!"

A New Look At Problems
Succeeding With Kids Who Can't, Won't, Or Don't
Succeeding With Kids Too Young To Write
What To Do When The Whole Lesson Is A Flop
Answers To Questions Teachers Ask Most Often

A NEW LOOK AT PROBLEMS

I imagine that you, too, have prodded the reluctant, confronted the disinterested, and winced at repeated (and probably whining) claims of, *"I can't think of anything!"* In every writing classroom, there are places and times when writing attempts proceed not-so-smoothly or lessons don't go according to plan. You can count on it! Things don't work the same every day, kids are different, problems and changes and interruptions and new wrinkles come up constantly.

The teaching of writing often feels like one ongoing juggling act. And that makes you the juggler—trying to keep a lot of stuff "in the air" at once, constantly keeping alert for the ball that goes higher than you planned, the object that falls more quickly than expected, or the new happening that comes flying in out of nowhere! This chapter offers help to iron out wrinkles, survive the days when nothing goes right, and handle situations that just plain baffle you.

> ### BIAS #26
> ### THE PROBLEM USUALLY IS **NOT** THE KIDS
> *Writing problems usually come from schedules, systems, approaches, assignments, or unrealistic expectations ... not from the writers.*

The best way to minimize problems with writing is to avoid them in the first place. The best way to do this is to **LISTEN TO YOUR WRITERS.** Look at the comments by writers at the beginning of this chapter. Just asking kids about writing can supply many clues about how to avoid trouble and make writing comfortable and successful.

When you do struggle with problems, it's also a good idea to stop and take a look at your own beliefs and attitudes.

194

How do you view those quirks and kinks in the writing-with-kids-process? You'll do best at juggling the problems that come up with writing if you consider...

... that PROBLEMS ARE NORMAL.

Everybody has periods of laziness or self-consciousness or disinterest in writing. I've had them all myself! There have been weeks when I didn't care if I ever finished this book, even though I believe strongly in the ideas and am committed to the writing of it. And sometimes a chapter has lain finished many days before I could bear to present it to my editor—because I get embarrassed when people read what I write. I believe you're in for frustrations if you expect every student to be eager to write during every writing session OR if you even expect yourself to be enthused at any given moment about writing.

... that PROBLEMS MAY NOT BE PROBLEMS AT ALL.

Frequently a student's apparent lack of success is only his lack of being on the same step of the process as someone else, or her hearing the beat of a different drum than some other writers. There are so many levels of writing ability and areas of interest that, in any one group, there are bound to be vast differences in the approaches to writing as well as in the kinds, quality, and complexity of finished products. **Take care not to see differences as problems.**

... that PROBLEMS ARE DESIRABLE.

Do you really prize diversity? If so, then resistance to writing in one form or on one topic or at a given moment will be WELCOMED. A writing session produces higher quality work when students are free to pursue options other than the initial suggestion. The discontent of one student with an assignment just may be the stimulus that propels the writer off in a better direction OR generates ten new ideas OR stretches your mind to create an alternative. Nine times out of ten, the lessons that "don't work" are the very ones that give birth to the most exhilarating and satisfying results.

SUCCEEDING WITH KIDS WHO CAN'T, WON'T, OR DON'T

You **will** encounter students who, out of fear, undeveloped motor skills, insecurity, boredom, disbelief, disinterest, weariness, distraction, stubbornness, hunger, or any number of other causes—will be unable or unwilling to write. One or several of these suggestions may help you to live comfortably with such incidents and to woo such individuals into successful writing growth.

1. **DON'T PANIC.**

   It'll be easier to find a good alternative or a workable solution if you're calm, warm, and reassuring—and particularly if you don't take the resistance as a personal affront.

2. **CONCENTRATE ON PEOPLE-BUILDING.**

   When someone feels good about himself or herself as a writer and thinker, willingness—and eagerness—to risk self-expression will increase. Any time that you dedicate to proving to kids their worth and ability will be hours well spent cementing the very foundations of written expression.

3. **SPEND MORE TIME ON ROMANCE.**

   When kids won't write, or think they can't, or don't want to—usually the reason is that they haven't been romanced sufficiently. Go back! Collect more ideas, read more examples, gather more words, OR spend several sessions with writers JUST on Stages 1 and 2—without going on to write.

4. **GIVE TIME OFF.**

   Respect the lack of interest in a topic or the low enthusiasm on a particular day and allow individuals to NOT write. If you're offering writing experiences often, an occasional day off won't hurt anyone's writing growth.

5. DON'T ANNOUNCE WRITING AHEAD OF TIME.

For a student who is already reluctant to write or nervous about it, fears will be compounded by a schedule on the chalkboard that says ... *Writing—Color Poetry—2:30 pm.* She'll have the whole day to build up resistance. Instead, **sneak into writing.** Start off with a fast-moving, non-threatening activity that gets students falling in love with an idea and scrawling down words, phrases, and sentences before they ever realize they're writing.

6. ENCOURAGE OTHER FORMS OF EXPRESSION.

Just as exposure to a virus doesn't guarantee catching it, so contact with joyful writing experiences doesn't cause writing fever for all students. For some, it is not—and never will be—the best means of communication. Some people just communicate better through other means, such as visual arts, music, and movement. Encourage expression in any form. And, remember, any communication will help to strengthen written expression.

7. GO BACK TO WORD PLAY.

Whatever your writers' ages or abilities, the foundation must be strong before the structure will be stable. ALL writers need to take time to fool around with words. Especially if writing is difficult or writers are insecure, take time to return to word play for solidifying the building blocks.

8. RETURN TO THE ORAL.

Instead of **writing** in Stage 4, **talk** through the rough draft. Students often gain fluency and confidence by forming their thoughts orally—then easing back into writing. Help students see that what they can say, they can write. Sometimes the best way is to let them talk while you jot down their ideas. Then you can actually show them: *"Here ... see how much you have to say? Now, you can write this down!"*

197

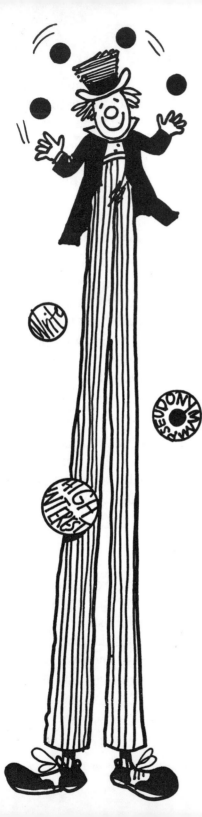

9. ACCENTUATE THE SHORT.

> **BIAS #27**
> **SMALL IS BEAUTIFUL**
>
> *The writing of short pieces makes success much more possible for students and allows for more effective teaching of writing techniques.*

Here is another of my strongest biases. New, reluctant, insecure, nervous, worried writers are more likely to succeed with short works (and are more willing to write) because the writing goes faster and there are fewer mistakes to correct. The rewards come more quickly. Actually, this is true of **all** writers, but particularly to be remembered for those who are struggling.

10. LET THEM WRITE UNDER A PSEUDONYM...

... and watch the tension dissolve! Kids are fascinated by the idea of writing with an invented name and are much more willing to write and share freely. Tell them stories about the lives and pseudonyms of some famous authors: Samuel Clemens (Mark Twain), Mary Ann Evans (George Eliot), and Charles Dodgson (Lewis Carroll). The volume of their writing increases amazingly as soon as kids start writing under a secret name.

11. THINK HIGH INTEREST & NON-THREATENING.

Try writing experiences about immediate concerns and common experiences—things kids know. Provide some of the words and phrases for them to use and combine. This allows them to ease into writing without the scary *thinking from scratch* part.

12. STOP THE REVISION FOR A WHILE.

It's the most intimidating part of the process for many writers. Try dropping it until expression loosens up. Just write—anything! If you must revise, do it on anonymous pieces only.

198

13. WRITE IN CLASS ... TOGETHER.

Success is the key for reluctant writers. They feel lost when assistance is too far away. Whenever you sense your writers are struggling alone—go back to writing together.

14. COMBINE WRITERS INTO PAIRS OR GROUPS.

Let kids write with a friend. Or invite older students in to assist a reluctant writer with a project OR **you** join a student having trouble and be the writing partner for a while. It's always easier to face a tough task with company, and two brainstormers will usually produce more ideas than a lone writer.

15. BEWARE BORING OR RIGID FORMS OR TOPICS.

Asking a young writer to comply with a tight form (a specific rhyme scheme, pattern, or number of syllables) sometimes makes the goal seem especially unattainable. Forcing forms that have no appeal to the individual threatens what little motivation might be there already. Making kids write on topics that have no interest or relevance to them does the same—only worse!

16. PROVIDE MORE DIRECTION.

Too many choices or too open an assignment can be confusing for unsure writers. Try giving more specifics—not to the whole group (unless they all need it), but to individuals. For instance...

Try putting a color in every line...
Start each line with ... **A place I'd never want to visit is...**

17. SEND THE KIDS TO A COMPUTER.

It never fails at our school: kids just write with less reluctance, more excitement, and greater success when they work at a keyboard. Knowing they can fuss with format, make the writing look clever, add graphics, make changes easily, and print out without re-copying really loosens up those uptight writers.

SUCCEEDING WITH KIDS TOO YOUNG TO WRITE

There hasn't been time for young writers to build fears or accumulate failures in writing. They are still awed by the magic of language. You can enjoy the delight of keeping that alive and fresh. Since your writers are too young to write lengthy pieces (or to write at all!), the time is free for spreading excitement about words, showing off the talents of language, and making communication easy and enjoyable.

To start the flow of expression, try these...

- **SENSITIZE** them to their environment. Get them to experience stuff with all five senses. Chew grass, catch snow, smell tacos, listen to butterflies, mimic animals, adopt different roles, compare steel wool to corduroy to silk. Touch and taste and smell and feel and watch and listen. And, as you do—share impressions and collect them in writing.

- **TALK** with them about their ideas, discoveries, wonderings, feelings. They have plenty of experiences on which to draw. Ask them to talk about:

    How does a lemon taste? What does it do to your tongue?

    How does it feel to have an ant crawl over your arm?

    Were you ever lost? How did you feel? What did you think?

- **TAPE RECORD** their answers to questions. Their cumulative statements and impressions will comprise a composition that can be written down by you or by an older child.

- **LISTEN** to songs, CDs, tapes. Sing along. Compose songs and poems and lyrics together or add verses to the songs you hear. Listen for rhythms and rhymes and special words in the music.

- **READ, READ, READ!** Let kids join in on refrains and short poems. Ask them to add different happenings or new endings or extra lines. Let them interpret as you read—by adding sound effects, clapping rhythms, or moving their bodies.

- **COMPOSE ORALLY.** Create lots of sentences, word groups, rhymes, riddles, questions, sayings. Sometimes, jot them down and read them back to the group. Hearing things they've created provides proof to them that they CAN write.

- **INVITE HELPERS** into your classroom to take dictations. Let young students dictate to an older student, a parent or adult friend, a senior citizen, the principal—anyone who can record the original material.

- **SHOW OFF** their writing after they've dictated it to you or someone else. They love to see their creations typed or enlarged on posters and banners. This makes great reading material too.

- **PAIR** each student with an older child to create a written piece together. Make it clear that each partner must contribute ideas.

- **EMPHASIZE** short pieces such as...

word collections	*riddles*	*questions*
short letters	*phrases*	*sentences*
captions	*jokes*	*poems*
descriptions	*titles*	*definitions*
directions	*similes*	*couplets*

WHAT TO DO WHEN THE WHOLE LESSON IS A FLOP

If the products are not what you'd hoped they'd be, OR if some or all of the students are disinterested or unmotivated or unchallenged, ask yourself—and ask your kids...

What are my expectations? Are they too high? Too low?
Is something being learned in the process in spite of the problems?
Am I smothering the joy of writing with too much editing?
Is the assignment too broad? Too narrow?
Is there enough direction? Is there too much?
Is the topic enticing and relevant? Boring? Irrelevant?
Did I treat the assignment with importance?
Did I skimp on time?
Have I chosen a time when kids are otherwise occupied or tired?
Was this too long an assignment?

THEN...

Modify your goals.
OR decide to concentrate on parts of the process and don't go on to a polished product for now.
OR take the topic in a different, more appealing direction.
OR ask students to suggest another topic.
OR provide more direction ... or less direction.
OR use the time for kids to write freely in journals.
OR put off this lesson until another time, when writers are ready.
OR give writers time to revisit, review, or organize their writing portfolios or their collections of unfinished stuff.
OR drop the idea all together. Do something other than writing.

ANSWERS TO QUESTIONS TEACHERS ASK MOST OFTEN

Q. When should writers go through the WHOLE process?

A. *Perhaps:* *every two or three times you write.*

Also: *when there's a good reason to go through all stages, such as when you're instructing students on how to polish pieces.*

Also: *when kids are particularly excited about a piece, or for any reason are anxious to have a precise draft.*

Less: *with younger, reluctant, or insecure writers.*

More: *with older or more advanced writers.*

Q. When should you NOT ask kids to rewrite?

A. *When:* *the piece doesn't need it. Sometimes the first draft is satisfying to the writer. Help kids recognize such times!*

Also: *when you're concentrating on just one of the stages.*

Also: *when a writer feels the first draft isn't important enough to her/him to be worth the revision time.*

Also: *when you need a break from revision for a while.*

But: *some writers will want to rewrite even when it's not required of them. By all means, let them do so.*

Q. How often should kids write?

A. *Try to do some kind of writing daily. (One way to encourage personal writing is have kids keep personal journals.)*

I recommend a teacher-initiated writing activity, mini-lesson for the class, or group-writing experience at least once a week, and more, if possible. Remember—writing doesn't have to be long to be good.

Q. I have to give a grade for writing on report cards. How do I decide?

A. *Design a clear plan for assessment that involves the students. If grades must be given, coordinate them to criteria for scoring and evaluating pieces of writing and writing portfolios. This can include such things as examining samples of writing over a period of weeks, watching and noting involvement in editing groups, keeping records on portfolio progress. Grades should reflect growth and involvement in the **whole writing process** and the student's development as a writer. (See Chapter 9.)*

Q. How do I get my kids to tolerate revising?

A. *The best way I know is to bring a real writer into the classroom to share his or her manuscripts and talk about the "fixing" or reworking that is a part of the writing.*

Other good ways are...

... doing the revision stages together.
... making it fun (ie: "Let's track down all the dull or inactive verbs! Who can find three?").
... easing into it in small steps.
... doing it on anonymous pieces of writing or pieces that the teacher wrote.
*... doing it on **short** pieces of writing (for quicker success).*
... making sure they don't have to do it every time they write.

Q. Do you always read EVERYTHING your students write?

A. *No! Kids should do lots of writing on their own that is shared with the teacher only if they choose. I certainly don't share all my writing with them or anybody else.*

And as for the response that writers need to their writing ... you are not the only valid responder. Other students, kids from other classes, parents, and volunteer helpers can read and respond to students' writing instead of the teacher.

Q. Should I write comments on all their pieces?

A. *NO ... often response may be given orally, casually—while looking over shoulders, during the sharing process, or in teacher-student conferences. And when you do give written responses, try not to mark up the writing. Give your comments on an attached index card or sticky note.*

*BUT ... **do** respond carefully and thoroughly some of the time to each writer—either in writing or in a one-to-one conference. Each writer deserves and needs this from the teacher.*

Q. I have a writing center in my room with many fun writing activities in it. But some of my students don't go there. How can I get them to use it?

A. *ASSIGN THEM! If a Writing Center or any other learning center is always optional, or kids think it's just a place to go to keep busy after their "real" work is done, all but the most eager writers won't use it.*

If you do have a Writing Center for independent writing...

... make sure there is a reason for kids to use it.
... make sure the activities there are relevant, interesting, and connected to your other writing instruction.
... make sure students know how and when and why to use it and what is expected of them in its use.

Q. Doesn't telling kids to write without stopping to correct just encourage mistakes in mechanics and other skills?

A. *The hurrying-to-get-your-thoughts-down-before-you-lose-them approach doesn't instill sloppiness in skills. The teacher is not saying to the writers, "Make mistakes freely." Tell kids to use the rules they know and spell the best they can. The idea is that you don't want to waste precious time stopping to labor over a word you can't spell or a rule you can't remember. You don't want to focus so hard on getting ideas in the proper sequence that you lose three other good ideas you could have included.*

Q. What should we do with the unfinished pieces?

A. *I'm for not throwing any writing away (unless, of course, a writer insists on getting rid of a particular piece). Because an incomplete idea today may be the nucleus for a masterpiece six months from tomorrow, it should be stored and guarded. Do this in a section of the writing portfolio you call "Good Ideas That Didn't Happen Yet." Have writers keep stuff they ...*

... don't like,
... lost interest in,
... gave up on,
... didn't have time to finish,
... want to work on later.

Let this collection become possible raw material for further writing or provide examples for future writing instruction...

> *Look through those unfinished pieces to see if you can find a phrase, sentence, or paragraph that uses effective voice.*

> *On Monday we'll be putting together a **Brag Bulletin**. Go through your "Unfinished Masterpieces" file and choose one piece of writing to polish. You'll have some time every day between now and then to get it ready for publication.*

Q. Should kids be allowed "poetic license"?

A. *Yes! ... as long as they know they're taking liberties with rules of mechanics. But don't forget that they need plenty of experiences with standard forms in addition to the experimental. If they're getting a grand variety of writing experiences, their skills won't suffer if they have fun now and then trying some unconventional things along with the conventional.*

HIGH-FLYING

Kids Take Poetic License

Q. What do you do with kids who include dirty words?

A. *Let them live with their own words.*
I find that kids do a lot of self-censoring or group-censoring. The objectionable words and phrases written for shock effect in the first draft usually disappear by the final draft.

And ... don't act impressed.
The teacher's horrified response somehow increases the life-span of inappropriate language.

And ... address it outright.
Tell kids, "This may be what you want to say, but it is not for publicizing at school. When you are an adult writer, it's up to you. Here, it's up to me."

Q. What do I do if I've tried everything and a student still can't think of anything to write?

A. *Find something non-disruptive for him to do while others write (but do involve him in the response stages).*

OR she can spend the time journal-writing private thoughts.

OR suggest that he be a class observer and keep a written record of what others are doing as they write.

AND stop worrying! If you have forty writing lessons during a year, and she misses half of them, she still will have had twenty valuable experiences. Besides, if she's in on the responding, revising, and sharing of others' works, she'll be growing even though she's not writing herself!

Q. What if I don't like writing? I mean, I really have a bad attitude!

A. *Don't teach it! It's not good for kids to miss out on writing instruction, but exposure to bad feelings about writing can be worse. If you just can't teach it without negatively affecting students, ask another teacher to hold writing sessions with your kids. In the meantime, get some training that will improve your own writing skills. It's the best way to turn you into a good teacher of writers.*

207

11

JUST IDEAS

"I always run out of ideas by October!"

Dreams ... In Broad Daylight
More Than 100 Alternatives To...
"What I Did On My Summer Vacation"
With Extra Pages Of:
Ideas Especially For Little Kids
Ideas Especially For Reluctant Writers
Ideas Especially For Gifted Writers
Ideas For Writing Across The Curriculum
Plus...4 More Good Ideas

dreams ... IN BROAD DAYLIGHT

More than *100* Alternatives to "What I Did On My Summer Vacation"

Dear Teacher,

The ideas in this chapter are directed at many different levels, interests, abilities, and topics. Most of them can be adapted to a different level by changing the examples, simplifying the directions, or adding more details.

Each idea is described BRIEFLY. None is developed as thoroughly here as it would need to be if used to begin a writing lesson. These are just beginnings—kernels. YOU and your students add the brainstorming, discussing, and collecting that help the kernels explode into writing!

FOUND WRITING

For anyone who doesn't feel like writing...here's a way to write without writing! Create...

poems	sentences
phrases	words
fables	announcements
letters	warnings
notes	questions
stories	secrets

...by cutting the words and letters from magazines or newspapers. It's a great way to send notes or anonymous messages.

HOW TO...

Write directions for how to...

make a banana split
eat with chopsticks
find the washroom
get bubblegum out of your hair
brush your teeth
make a rainbow
pet a lion
operate a computer
create a rap song
get peanut butter off the roof of
your mouth

DREAMS

How do you fall asleep? Do you wander around in your sleep? What are your dreams like? Do you dream in color? Are there conversations in your dreams? Are there other people (or creatures) lurking around?

Write a script from one of your dreams.

OR...write a poem wherein every line begins...*I dreamed...*

OR...describe a recurring dream...

You can write dream poems in lots of shapes. Try some different ones.

EPITAPHS

Write some silly epitaphs:

Here lies Maryanne Doe
She tripped on a toothpick
And broke her toe.

At rest here is John Bloom
Our neighbor of late.
He brushed with Crest
But should've used Colgate.

Can you write one for:

Peter Pan? a plumber?
a snake who got bit by a
poisonous lady?

LOVE STORIES

Write about unusual romances...such as between...

a tennis shoe and a potato peel
a bee and a mathematician
a doctor and a bandage

Tell how the relationship developed.

CRAZY COMBINATIONS

Write a poem that has in every line...
an animal and a kitchen utensil
a kind of shoe and a vegetable
a body part and a famous person
a tool and a food
a pasta and a dance

OR any other crazy combinations!

FIRST CLASS MAIL

When you're in the mood for writing a letter, write to...

...your congresswoman or man...giving your opinion on some issue
...an animal you'd like to convince to be your pet
...someone whose name you've chosen from your mom's address book
...the principal... telling something you think he or she should know
...yourself from yourself
...yourself as if it were coming from someone in the future or past

Write to thank someone...to apologize...to request...to complain...
to cheer someone up...to explain...to question...to protest...to surprise!

YOU'RE INVITED

Write an invitation to any sort of an event ...serious or silly...real or imaginary...in the present, past, or future. Tell the guests when it starts and ends, what to expect, what to wear and bring. Invite someone to...

a ladybug hunt   *World War II*
a safari   *an alligator hunt*
a trip on an alien space ship
a wild river raft trip
a boomerang throwing contest
the Battle of Gettysburg

WRITER'S MARATHON

Have a marathon in your class or join with another class. Set a starting time for people to begin writing. Agree on requirements and prizes for the person (or class) who writes the longest...or the most pieces...or the greatest variety. Kids might work in teams, with each member creating a different genre. You'll need to make up your own rules to fit the schedules, ages, abilities, and interests of your marathoners.

COME TO YOUR SENSES!

Choose a human emotion or any other idea. Think about experiencing it with all five senses. Write a line that tells what color it is. Then write some other lines to describe it using just one of the senses.

Joy is bright green	*(color)*
It tastes like orange juice	*(taste)*
It smells like sunshine	*(smell)*
And reminds me of fireworks	*(sight)*
It sounds like a crackling fire	*(sound)*
Joy makes me feel like giggling	*(feel)*

Mary Lee Fiacco, Grade 2

NO-PREPARATION SPEECHES

You have three minutes to prepare for a one-minute speech. Write notes to yourself for the ideas or points you'll want to include in the speech. Here are some speech topics...

What to do when you've swallowed a Junebug
Why anyone would want to be president
Ten good uses for a pocket
How to show anger without getting in trouble
Situations to avoid
Why you should try hang gliding

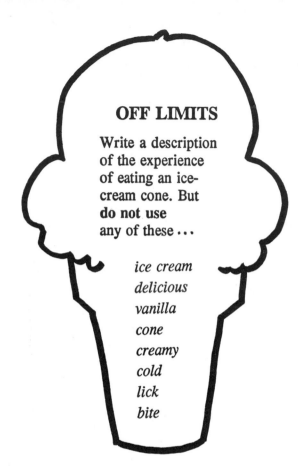

OFF LIMITS

Write a description of the experience of eating an ice-cream cone. But **do not use** any of these ...

ice cream
delicious
vanilla
cone
creamy
cold
lick
bite

THINGS I KNOW

Write about what you know. You can start each line with **I know**...or do the writing in any form or genre. Just keep to the subject of showing off some thing or things you know. (Anything from *I know how to tie my shoes.* .to...*I know all about quadratic equations.*)

I'VE GOT A COMPLAINT

Pretend that you are in charge of the complaint department at a grocery store...ice-cream parlor...a kite shop...skateboard shop...pet store...pizza place...barber...computer store...music store...or any other store. Write a list of the possible complaints you might receive. For each one have ready a possible answer or explanation.

GOSSIP GALORE

Write a gossip column about fictitious people or the people in your school. Include only the kind of gossip that won't be likely to hurt people's feelings or embarrass them.

EAVESDROPPING

Listen in on any conversation. Write down their words as accurately as you can. Don't try this one too often...or you could get into trouble!

TALL TALES

Write a story about a happening in a way that stretches the facts a little or a lot. Do your writing on a piece of adding machine tape that you've turned the long way. Mount the tall tale on black paper and attach legs to make it very tall.

A PLACE YOU'LL WANT TO VISIT

Write a pamphlet or brochure that will sell someone on the idea of joining a trip or visiting an unusual place...

a medieval castle

a kids-only resort

a diet ranch

a raft trip down the Amazon River

a newly-discovered volcano

Ali Baba's cave or the inside of Aladdin's lamp

the inside of a whale

DON'T WRITE MORE THAN ONE SENTENCE

You only get **one** sentence to do this. It can be a statement or a question, exclamation or quote—but only one! The sentence must...*describe...OR compare...OR contrast...OR persuade... OR explain... OR evaluate...OR joke about.*

CLIFF-HANGERS

Hang a long piece of paper from a hanger. On the paper, write the beginning of an exciting story. Don't finish the story!

STOP right at a breathtaking spot. Then hang your story in a place where someone else can finish it. You finish another person's cliff-hanger.

ON THE TRACK OF BIGFOOT

Write a list of Bigfoot words: words that someone could use in telling a tale about Bigfoot... sound, smell, sight and feeling words.

OR

Make a list of ten reasons why people might believe in Bigfoot and ten reasons why they might not.

OR

Prepare notes for a speech that will convince someone to believe in Bigfoot. Make a mask, costume, puppet, movie, or drawing to use with your speech.

LOOKING FOR TROUBLE?

Write warnings that caution people against possible hazards...real or imaginary...silly or serious...in your school...home... in the streets ...on the school bus...at a circus...in a lion's cage...at a high school dance...or anywhere else you believe there may be risks or hazards.

YOU'RE BEING FOLLOWED!

Follow someone around, or carefully watch a person for a week, keeping notes on that person's activities, feelings, behaviors, reactions. At the end of the week write up a summary for your *private detective* report. (Don't give away anything confidential!) Share your report with other detectives. See if you can guess who the person is that the other detective was following.

214

DOES THE NAME FIT?

Make up names for characters you see in pictures. Make the names match the qualities that you think you see.

OR

Without using pictures, create names and write descriptions of persons to fit the names. Tell how the name connects to the person's life or activities.

RE-PRINTS

Find a picture you like. Write a very precise description of the picture. Then give your written description to another student. **(Do not show the picture!)** Ask that person to try to re-create the picture by drawing according to your description. Then...compare the drawings with the originals! This will show you how accurate a description you wrote.

ODES

An ode is a praise to someone or something. Write an ode to...

...*your calculator*
...*peanut butter*
...*your soccer ball*
...*pizza*
...*your old sneaker*
...*curly hair*
...*a toothbrush*
...*the end of summer*
...*your childhood*

HOW TO TELL...

Explain...seriously, or with some touches of humor...how someone could tell that one of these things has happened or is happening...

a tornado
a nosebleed
an argument between adults
chicken pox
a blizzard
a math test

WAKE UP!

Invent and describe a product that would be guaranteed to wake up anybody in the morning. Write an advertisement for your invention. Be sure that the ad describes the invention clearly and tells all of its merits. You might create a drawing or model to illustrate your new product.

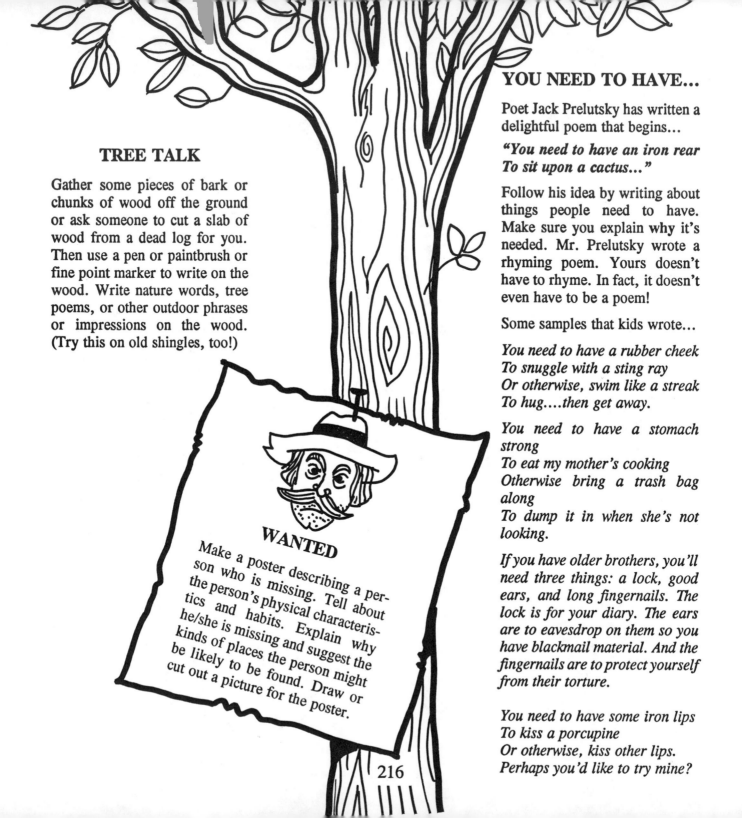

TREE TALK

Gather some pieces of bark or chunks of wood off the ground or ask someone to cut a slab of wood from a dead log for you. Then use a pen or paintbrush or fine point marker to write on the wood. Write nature words, tree poems, or other outdoor phrases or impressions on the wood. (Try this on old shingles, too!)

WANTED

Make a poster describing a person who is missing. Tell about the person's physical characteristics and habits. Explain why he/she is missing and suggest the kinds of places the person might be likely to be found. Draw or cut out a picture for the poster.

216

YOU NEED TO HAVE...

Poet Jack Prelutsky has written a delightful poem that begins...

*"You need to have an iron rear
To sit upon a cactus..."*

Follow his idea by writing about things people need to have. Make sure you explain why it's needed. Mr. Prelutsky wrote a rhyming poem. Yours doesn't have to rhyme. In fact, it doesn't even have to be a poem!

Some samples that kids wrote...

*You need to have a rubber cheek
To snuggle with a sting ray
Or otherwise, swim like a streak
To hug....then get away.*

*You need to have a stomach strong
To eat my mother's cooking
Otherwise bring a trash bag along
To dump it in when she's not looking.*

If you have older brothers, you'll need three things: a lock, good ears, and long fingernails. The lock is for your diary. The ears are to eavesdrop on them so you have blackmail material. And the fingernails are to protect yourself from their torture.

*You need to have some iron lips
To kiss a porcupine
Or otherwise, kiss other lips.
Perhaps you'd like to try mine?*

THE WAY WE WERE

Write anecdotes or poems or diary entries about your younger days. Tell…

The worst thing that ever happened to me
The last time I sassed my mother
When Mr. Albertson tripped on my skateboard
The time my lizard got loose at church
My first day in kindergarten

REAL ESTATE AGENTS

Borrow some old house descriptions from a realtor. Watch the newspapers to see what houses are for sale and to read the information written about them. Write up descriptions of some houses for your own file. Try your house or a friend's. Can you write one for your secret clubhouse, your school, your classroom, or a local store that would convince someone to see it as a great buy?

SIX REASONS

Write six reasons…

for tomatoes
for not wearing shoes
why people eat
for having a pet
why I don't feel like writing
for eating vegetables
why friends have fights
for falling in love

ENCYCLOPEDIA POEMS

Choose several interesting facts from the encyclopedia. Use one or more of them as a line or a theme for a joke…a poem…a news report…a diary entry…an adventure story…an ad for marshmallows…etc.
OR turn the whole encyclopedia entry into a riddle or poem.

BORROWED STARTERS

Borrow a line from…

a poem
or a title from a book
to serve as the starting line
for your own story
or movie script
or poem
or description

…to use in your own writing. It will help you get a good start on an idea.

DIAMANTE

A diamante is a diamond-shaped poem that tells about opposites. Start with a pair of opposites such as day-night, new-old, tall-short, etc.

Lines 1 and 7 name the opposites.
Lines 2 and 6 each give two adjectives describing the opposite nearest it.
Lines 3 and 5 give three participles (**ing** words) describing the nearest opposite.
Line 4 is in the middle. It changes from the first idea to the opposite by giving two nouns for each. See the example below. Notice how the poem changes from one theme to the opposite:

BORING
Dull, dreadful
Dragging, deadening, stifling
Nothing, blankness, curiosity, something
Awakening, exciting, captivating
Noticable, brilliant
AWESOME

DAY
Bright, colorful
Opening, moving, waking
Sunrise, sunshine, shadows, sunset
Closing, slowing, sleeping
Dark, colorless
NIGHT

217

ESCAPE PLAN

Write a plan telling someone how to get out of a sticky, difficult, or perhaps dangerous situation...such as...having accidentally wandered into the hippo's cage at the zoo...or having bubblegum stuck in your hair...or being caught wearing your mother's best sweater...or locking yourself out of the house in the middle of the night...or having blue lips and a blue tongue when your dad is wondering what happened to his piece of blueberry pie... or realizing that the shadow you keep seeing in the water near your floating raft (with you on it) is the shape of a shark.

BACKWARDS BEASTS

Turn around the name of any animal and you'll have an interesting, unusual beast as a subject for a short tale or rhyme. How would a *Noil* or an *Olaffub* or an *Elidocorc* look, sound and behave? Choose an animal name and turn it around to find the beast's name. Then, use some fabric scraps or wallpaper scraps to create the beast. After you know what it looks like, write about it...

*The **raeb** is a nasty beast*
All black with shaggy hair.
Frontwards, not scary in the least
He's just a cuddly (bear) .

The scary, sneaky ekans
Has legs and arms with spiky fans
Backwards it's an awful fake
Forward it's a slinky (snake) .

*The **tarrop** has such awful teeth*
Three up above, and six beneath.
Turn her around, give her a carrot
She's a friendly, chatty (parrot) .

Don't take a gip to lunch
His appetite's so big
He might have the table to munch
After all, he's really a (pig) .

HOME REMEDIES

Write remedies for...common (or uncommon) diseases...illnesses... ailments...or minor accidents likely to happen around home or school. They can be serious or ridiculous.

How to get rid of freckles
How to cure a broken heart
The fastest cure for a sore throat
How to get rid of a bully
The best remedy for bad grades
How to live with a big nose

MY LAST WILL

After reading some examples of real wills, write (in language that sounds legal) what stuff of yours you wish to will to...the school...the teacher...or the new students...as you leave your class and move on to the next grade or a new school.

218

HOW?

LOOK
at a person's face...what does it tell you...
about the way she is feeling?
what he's thinking?
where she's going?
what he's like?

NOTICE
facial expressions
body language (posture, movement, mannerisms)
clothing (type, fit, purpose, color)
friendliness (interaction with others)

WONDER
What is this person doing?
Is it work or play or what?
How does he seem to feel about what he is doing?
Does he notice other people? Talk to others?
Is she in a world by herself?
How does she react to the other people or situations?
What do you think you could learn from following
    or watching this person?
Of what places, sounds, songs, colors, feelings, ideas
    does this person remind you? Why?

People Watching

WHO?

pet owners	babies	giving
preachers	shy people	taking
secretaries	tall people	fighting
pilots	show offs	eating
birdwatchers	skinny people	hiking
friends	old people	relaxing
lovers	young people	hurting
teachers		sharing
actors	**PEOPLE...**	smiling
drivers		scowling
athletes	working	waiting
neighbors	moping	doing nothing
motorcyclists	playing	
joggers	sleeping	anybody...
strangers	thinking	
adults	crying	
	helping	

WHERE?

ski slopes	car washes
streets	swimming pools
parking lots	car dealers
stores	movies
traffic jams	schools
ball games	concerts
libraries	on television
homes	hotels
weddings	funerals
bus stations	restaurants
markets	parties
in lines	in other cars
through windows	banks
carnivals	fairs
parks	zoos
jails	plays
museums	phone booths
trains	buses
in strollers	hospitals
offices	playgrounds
elevators	churches
barber shops	shoe stores
assemblies	doctors' offices

anywhere . . .

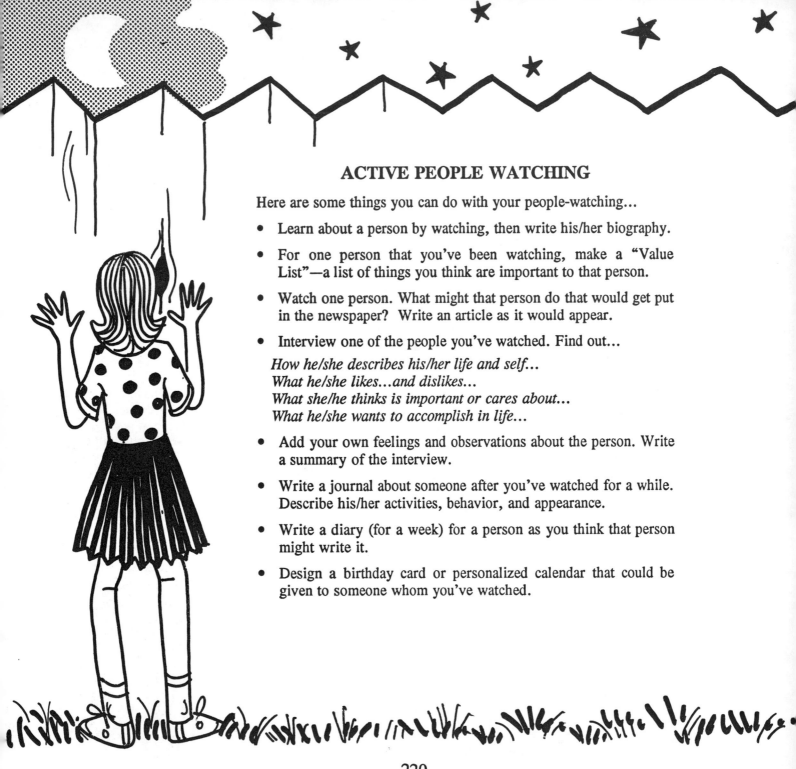

ACTIVE PEOPLE WATCHING

Here are some things you can do with your people-watching...

- Learn about a person by watching, then write his/her biography.

- For one person that you've been watching, make a "Value List"—a list of things you think are important to that person.

- Watch one person. What might that person do that would get put in the newspaper? Write an article as it would appear.

- Interview one of the people you've watched. Find out...

  How he/she describes his/her life and self...
  What he/she likes...and dislikes...
  What she/he thinks is important or cares about...
  What he/she wants to accomplish in life...

- Add your own feelings and observations about the person. Write a summary of the interview.

- Write a journal about someone after you've watched for a while. Describe his/her activities, behavior, and appearance.

- Write a diary (for a week) for a person as you think that person might write it.

- Design a birthday card or personalized calendar that could be given to someone whom you've watched.

220

PEOPLE ARE THE WORLD'S GREATEST RESOURCE

Catch the people-watching fever! You can learn a lot about human behavior, interpersonal relationships, values, occupations...and find out about what makes people be people!

- Invite people to come to the classroom so that you can watch them doing what they like to do. Invite...

  an artist to sculpt or paint or draw
  a jeweler to repair a watch
  a grandmother to crochet
  an upholsterer to re-upholster a chair
  a dancer to rehearse
  an electrician to repair an out-of-order socket
  a songwriter to work on a song

- After you observe a person working, write a job description of that person's work.

- Write a collection of jokes or riddles or quotations about people you've watched.

- As you watch and eavesdrop on people, collect impressions, ask questions, and take notes. Then combine your impressions into a series of poems about people.

- Create a collage with pictures you've found of people just being people. Give it a title.

- Watch a person for 15 minutes. Write a secret you think he/she might be keeping.

- Design and describe a friend for someone you've watched.

- Make up a name, lifestyle, and daily routine for someone you've been watching.

"ME" STUFF

Write a poem in which every other line begins:

I seem to be _____

But I really am _____

OR like this...

I'm good at _____

I'm not so good at _____

Finish this:

I am _____

I am _____

I am _____

I am _____

I am _____

For kids too young to write a full autobiography, a simpler form can be substituted. Try "PICTO-biographies." Bring in some old photos and recent photos of yourself and your family, pets, friends, etc. Paste the pictures in any order you wish on a long piece of paper. For each picture, write or dictate a sentence that tells about some piece of your life that's shown in that picture.

Draw around your hand. Cut out the outline. On your hand write all the things that you can do with your hands.

Design a flag for yourself. Make it any shape, size, and colors you want. On the flag, write words or phrases or sentences that tell about things or ideas in which you believe.

Have someone (the teacher or another adult or student) draw a silhouette of your head's profile while you sit in front of a light from a filmstrip projector. "Catch" the shadow on dark paper and draw around it. Cut out the silhouette. Glue words on it that have something to do with yourself.

Lie down on the floor on a piece of mural paper. Have a friend draw around your body. Cut yourself out! Then write the story of your life or personal anecdotes on the cut-out of yourself.

Write some words that describe yourself on an old belt to make a *ME-belt*. If you don't have an old belt, you can make one out of fabric scraps. (You could also try a *ME-sock, glove, slipper, shoe,* or any other item of clothing, for that matter!)

Find a box that has six sturdy sides. Tape any flaps down so that it is a perfect and closed box. Cover all the sides with white or colored paper. Write or draw or paste something about yourself on each side of the box to form a *ME-cube*. Possibilities...

    snapshots
    favorite words
    color poems you've written
    your autobiography
    your family tree
    your handprint or footprint
    autographs of your favorite people
    cut-out pictures of things that tell about you

Make a *ME-mobile* by hanging some of these things from a hanger: pictures, words, writing, and anything else that tells about **YOU**. Punch a hole in each item and suspend it from the hanger with string.

ESPECIALLY, but not only, for little kids

BEASTLY BEGINNINGS

Imagine, create (with paint or paper or anything else), and describe (with words) an imaginary creature. Tell or write a story about its habits and adventures.

HELLO, OPERATOR?

Tell or write what you would say on the telephone if you were calling...

the library to find if they have a book that you want
the president to tell your opinion on one of his policies
a theater to check the time of a movie
your mother at work to tell her about how the supper slid
   down the drain

FOG WALK

Watch for an especially foggy day. Take a walk to feel the air...and smell and taste and touch the fog. Write down some words and capture some phrases that can be used in fog poems. (Try a walk on a rainy or snowy or windy or muggy day, too.)

SALES PITCH

With your classmates, gather and bring to school empty cans, boxes, or bags from all sorts of products. Choose a product and prepare a sales pitch that will convince others to buy and use the product. Then write an ad or make a poster that will accomplish the same purpose.

LOST AND FOUND

Take something out of your school's or class's lost and found box. Write a clue that tells one thing you know (from looking at the item) about its owner. Read your clue to the class...it may help find the right owner.

JUMP ROPE JINGLES

Create jingles, rhymes, or little stories to say while you jump rope. Start with a line the teacher gives you—or add a few lines to a jump rope rhyme you already know.

There are many good collections of jump rope rhymes and jingles available at local book stores and libraries.

A-B-C BOOKS

Bring lots of alphabet books into the classroom. Read them all to get ideas about how *Alphabet Books* are written and presented. Then...each student can choose one letter of the alphabet. (Decide on this with the group so that all the letters get chosen.) For that letter, write some words and draw a picture (or a few) to make the page for that letter. Then...put it together with the other alphabet pages to make a class *A-B-C Book*.

SUPER SNOOPERS

Hide something in your classroom. Choose something small enough to be easily hidden but large enough to be found. Then write careful and simple directions for someone to follow that will lead to the treasure. Kids can trade directions with each other and go searching.

TASTING PARTY

Bring samples of some tasty things to school. Try to get a variety of different tastes for your group. Set up stations with a different tasting item at each. Visit the stations, writing down words and phrases and similes for each taste. Try a smelling party, too!

YOUNG GOURMETS

Tell someone how to prepare your favorite food. Ask that person to write down the recipe while you dictate it. A collection of these from your whole class makes a nice present for you to give on a holiday (Mother's Day!).

STRETCHED

Tell some lies and stretched stories about things that could never really happen. Then cut large rubber band so that it lies flat. Write your lie on it. See how BIG it looks when it is all stretched out.

IN THE BAG!

Choose one thing to put into a small paper lunch bag. Staple it shut! Pass it around to everyone in the class. They may feel the item through the bag...but cannot open it. Ask them to write words on the outside of the bag that tell about the item. Then... open the bag, and with eyes closed, feel the item and write more words.

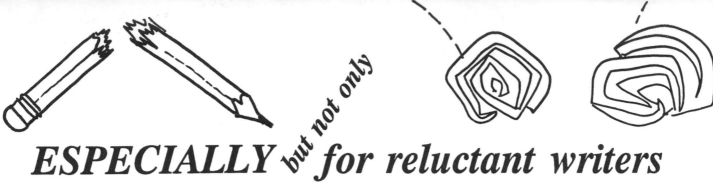

ESPECIALLY *but not only* for reluctant writers

PASS IT ON

Sit in a circle with the whole class. When the leader says, *START,* write a good beginning for an adventure story. When the leader says, *PASS,* pass your paper to the right. Then...read the beginning that the last person wrote and write a good middle to the story. When the leader says, *PASS,* again, send your story along to the right. This time, add a strong ending to the story you receive. When it is time to pass again, add a title to the new paper that you get. Then share the final *Pass-Along Stories* with the whole group.

10 THINGS

Make a list of any of the ideas below or any other list of...**10 Things**...

...to do last
...to do first
...never to do
...I don't understand
...to change
...to keep secret
...to do before breakfast
...I'll never forget
...I'd like to forget
...I'll never regret
...to do before leaving high school
...about teeth
...to do before breakfast
...to do slowly
...to do in a hurry
...you should try

____ MAKE ____

A	A
LIST	LIST
OF	OF
10	10
THINGS	THINGS
TO	TO
WHICH	WHICH
YOU	YOU
WOULD	WOULD
SAY	SAY

"YES" "NO"

REVISED COPY

Revise nursery rhymes to make them contemporary. OR...rewrite a well-know story so that it is written in language simple enough for younger children.

NUTS

Crack open a walnut carefully so that you don't break either half. Remove the meat of the nut. Then write an idea for a *nutty starter* (or a joke or riddle or silly tale) and put it inside the shell. Glue the shell back together. Hang the nut on a dead tree branch so someone else can pick it and use it to begin some writing. Some samples...

the tooth fairy that gets sick at the sight of teeth
a rock band made up of singing bananas
a flea with a pet giant
a can opener that's taking over the world

PHOETRY

Phoetry is a combination of **poetry** and **photography**. Bring photographs or take pictures of anything that interests you. Then write poetry to describe the actions, impressions, feelings, experiences, or places represented in the pictures.

WOULD YOU BELIEVE?

Tell or write lies...really big whoppers...about the weather, fishing trips, things you've done, people, eating, anything!

It was so hot that.....
He was so fast that.....
Yesterday was colder than.....
You'll never believe that I.....

SECRETS

Write secret messages with invisible ink (lemon juice or vinegar or apple juice). Do the writing with a small brush or cotton swab or your finger. Pass the secrets to a friend when the writing is dry. Your friend can decipher the words by holding the paper close to a hot light bulb. The writing will turn brown so it can be read.

WORD BOWL

Fill a bowl with interesting words. Then pass the bowl so that each student can choose one (or two or three) without looking. Use your words as starters for a joke or story or poem. OR...use them in a title. You might combine words with a friend and work together. Sometimes it is fun to work as a whole class to try using all the chosen words in one piece of writing.

TRANSLATIONS

Find a poem that is written in a foreign language. "Translate" it by writing what you **think** the words might say...

CROSSWORDS BACKWARDS

Give students a crossword puzzle that is already filled in. Ask them to write the clues for each word.

Schneeflockehen, weibrockchen,
  Wann kommst du geschneit?
Du wohnst in der wolke,
  Dein weg ist so weit.
Komm, setz ditch ans fenster,
  Dulievlicher stern,
  Malst blumen und blatter.
Wir haben dich gern.

Sally, Willy,
  want to come to school?
You stay on the walk
  or your feet are so wet.
Don't set the desk on fire,
  the teacher is mean,
  mostly he yells and blabbers
When you have your desk gone.

RAMBLING MINDS

When you are having a hard time concentrating on one idea for writing, write in **a stream of consciousness** style. That means...let your pencil follow your mind! Just write about anything and everything that comes into your mind—even if the ideas are not related to each other. Later, you might pick out one of those ideas and concentrate on it for writing something.

227

ESPECIALLY,
but not only, for gifted writers

HIDE-A-WORD

Write interesting words on little pieces of paper. Fold and staple them. Write, **Top Secret,** on the outside of each one. Pass a word to each student. The task is to write a paragraph (or any other short form of writing) in which the word is hidden. The idea is to make that word as inconspicuous as possible. After the writing is done, students can read the pieces aloud to the class. The class tries to guess which word was the one that the writer was trying to hide.

MONOLOGUES

Monologues are grand speeches you make to the world OR...to someone in particular from the safe position of being absolutely alone with no one to hear...and especially...no one to interrupt. Write one to express your thoughts or the thoughts of another real or fictitious person.

UNDER INSPECTION

The next time you go to a restaurant, an office, a video store, or a ball game... pretend to be an official **inspector**.

Take notes on the quality of the food, the service, the cleanliness, the safety, the quality of the performance. Write a summary of your findings. If you are brave enough, share your report with the establishment.

HOW IS A DUCK LIKE A STOMACH ACHE?

See if you can make some unusual comparisons like these. For each one, be ready to explain why you are comparing the two things (What do they have in common?).

Fresh air and potato chips are alike because _____

A goldfish is as _____ *as a math test because* _____

Losing a friend is as _____ *as riding a roller coaster.*

I am like _____ *because* _____
    (a food)

AT SECOND GLANCE

Rewrite a well-known story from the viewpoint of a different character than the one who is the *STAR* in the original version. For example...

Tell about Red Riding Hood's experience from the wolf's viewpoint.

Describe Thanksgiving Dinner from the point of view of the turkey or the pig.

Re-tell the story of JAWS from the shark's view.

SYNESTHESIA

Think about things that are usually perceived by one sense (sight, hearing, smell, etc.) as they would seem when perceived through a different sense. Write about...

how yellow might smell...or a sandwich might sound...or how a plan tastes...or what a noise feels like...or how pain looks...

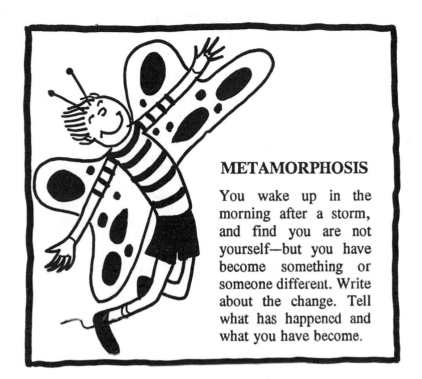

METAMORPHOSIS

You wake up in the morning after a storm, and find you are not yourself—but you have become something or someone different. Write about the change. Tell what has happened and what you have become.

POETRY, POETRY, HERE, THERE, EVERYWHERE

Start with a news article or an advertisement or the label of a box or an argument or a TV dialogue...and turn it into a poem. Use the same information and ideas, but write them in poetic form. (REMEMBER...poetry does not have to rhyme.)

QUOTATIONS BARTLETT NEVER HEARD

Collect interesting quotes from all kinds of sources...books you've read... classmates...friends ...people in the halls...magazines...folks on buses...etc. Try to include many kinds of quotes from many kinds of people and places. Add your own quotes and print or type up your own collection into a booklet.

YELLOW, YELLOW PAGES

Make a directory of all the goods and services available within your school. Write an ad for each one and create alphabetical entries for them all. Don't forget to include the talents of the students. Compile these into your own yellow pages. Print them up on yellow paper. See the telephone book's yellow pages for a sample.

WRITING Across The Curriculum...

> Look for writing opportunities in every other discipline or activity. After all, poetry and prose are made of life's experiences...so history, geometry, language, physical activity, science, art, music, and all other areas of study stir impressions, issues, ideas, and responses that can be expressed in words.

ART

MIX...

... **CHANTS** with sand paintings

... **MYSTERIES** with a shadow show

... **BIOGRAPHIES** with portraits

... **VALUE STATEMENTS** with totem poles

... **SPOOKY TALES** with black crayon resists

... **SNOW POETRY** with soap bubble paintings

... **COLOR WORDS or PHRASES** with batik

... **MONSTER TALES** with squished paint blobs

... **CHARACTER SKETCHES** with cartoon sketches

... **WIND POEMS** with pinwheels or wind chimes

... **HAIKU** with silkscreens or bamboo painting

... **PICTURESQUE PHRASES** with torn paper scenes

... **EARTH POETRY** with rock painting or mud painting

... **DESCRIPTIONS OF SCENES** with wet watercolor paintings

... **LIES or TALL TALES** with oversized, exaggerated creatures

... **LIMERICKS** with crazy gourd characters or vegetable people

... **POEMS about FEELINGS** with melted crayon or wet chalk designs

... **PROVERBS** with clay plaques or wood collages or stained glass designs

... **TALES about PEOPLE** with paper-mache or clay-sculpted masks

... **CITY POEMS or OBSERVATIONS ON CITY LIFE** with skyline paintings

... **IMPRESSIONISTIC POETRY** with paper mosaics or crayoned pointillism

... **AUTOBIOGRAPHIES or ME-POEMS** with body outlines or face silhouettes

... **ECOLOGY POSTERS or ECOLOGICAL BUMPER STICKERS** with junk scul

Chants
CARTOONS
Silkscreen
Poems
BATIK
BUMPER STICKERS
Posters
Totem Poles
Portraits
CREATURES
Monster Tales
MASKS
Junk Sculpture
HAIKU
Silhouettes
Mysteries

... Plan a **NEW BUSINESS** or develop a **NEW PRODUCT** or offer a **NEW SERVICE**...then...

design packaging	create advertisements
write contracts	form job descriptions
make up slogans	make lists of perspective customers
write jingles	write a resume of your services
prepare a catalog	invent a business name and logo

... Write **BIRTH CERTIFICATES** for famous figures in history.

... Write **ANNOUNCEMENTS** for events that happened in the past.

... Write **ROLE EXPECTATIONS**...describing expectations for behaviors for persons in various roles within social groups.

... Compile a **SCRAPBOOK of FAMILY HISTORY,** including a family tree and interesting information about your heritage. Write **LETTERS** to relatives to gain the information.

... Make a **TIME LINE** showing major events and influences in your life or in the life of a current or past historical figure.

... Keep a **CULTURAL VALUES NOTEBOOK.** Find pictures that demonstrate or represent particular values held by a culture. (You can include a variety of different cultures.) For each picture, write words or sentences to explain what the picture shows.

... Create a **PHOTO ESSAY** on a person or situation in current events.

... Write a **GOSSIP COLUMN** from history, telling about figures from the past...as a newspaper back then might have told it.

... Turn a current event (or past event) into a **TALL TALE.**

... Write **TRAVEL BROCHURES**...for any place...here or there...now or in the past. Include interesting information about the culture, characteristics, attractions, and geography of the place.

... Develop a **FLAG, SEAL, SYMBOL, PLEDGE or NATIONAL ANTHEM** for a new country.

... Write a **TRIBUTE** to the Red Cross or any other social organization that has played a part in current or past world events.

... Create a **PROTECT-YOUR-ENVIRONMENT HANDBOOK** for children, telling ways that young people can contribute to the wise use and preservation of the earth's resources.

... "Paint" a **WORD PORTRAIT** of friendship. Interview different kinds and ages of people to gather ideas about what friendship means.

SOCIAL STUDIES

flag
seal
anthem
certificates
photo essays
scrap book
travel brochures
tributes
word portraits
gossip column

... Write **DIRECTIONS** for an original math game that will help players learn math facts.

... Make up **JUMP ROPE RHYMES** using multiplication facts.

... Write a **SPEECH** that will convince folks to love algebra.

... Create imaginative **WORD PROBLEMS** for others to solve. Use names and real situations of classmates in the problems.

... Write a **LOVE STORY** between a circle and a trapezoid.

... Write a **POEM** using at least 10 math words or concepts.

... Create a **PLAY** about a math concept. *(Zany Zero,* or *Peg's Problems with Probability* or *Infinity Goes Hawaiian.)*

... Write an **AUTOBIOGRAPHY** of a scalene triangle.

... Write a **DIET** for an overweight ton.

... Write up a **CONTRACT** between yourself and someone who is buying your snow board on time payments (with interest).

... Create a **MENU** for a restaurant where a family of four big eaters could eat dinner for under $15.00.

MATH

... Write **COUPLETS** that will help you remember addition facts.

... Make a *NO NUMBER* **BOOKLET** telling what the world would be like without numbers.

... Write **SONG LYRICS and MUSIC** to explain how division works.

... Make a *MATH DICTIONARY* with your definitions of math terms.

... Write an **ODE** to the number 17 or any other number you choose.

... Make **SIGNS, POSTERS** and **ADVERTISING BILLBOARDS** telling about the assets of a math concept.

... Make a *DIRECTORY of METRIC MEASURES*. Explain the metric system so that your directory could be used by someone unfamiliar with the system.

... Design a **BOOK JACKET** for your math book...or an **INDEX**...or a **TABLE OF CONTENTS**...or write a **REVIEW** of the book.

... Design a **MATH AMUSEMENT PARK** where all the attractions have something to do with math. Write a **TRAVEL BROCHURE** describing the park and enticing people to come.

232

... Make a **RECIPE BOOK** giving menus for well-balanced meals for a family.

... Write the **LIFE STORY** of a jellyfish or tadpole.

... Write a **SCHEDULE** for the care and feeding of the classroom pet (or a pet at home).

... Make a **DIRECTORY** of common diseases. Describe symptoms and cures for each.

... Write a **RESUME** of your qualifications to be the class computer specialist or zoo-keeper or plant custodian.

... Write a **TRIBUTE** to your teeth, vocal chords, muscles, hair, esophagus, liver, spleen, joints, or bones.

... Write **SEQUENTIAL DIRECTIONS** for making a bug-catcher, identifying an insect, preserving animal tracks, or making an electrical circuit.

... Write a **TONGUE TWISTER** about tongues or tendons.

... Write a *BOOK of SCIENCE & SUPERSTITIONS*, telling superstitions and opposing scientific explanations.

SCIENCE

... As you study the universe, create **SPACE FANTASIES**.

... Write a **TABLE OF CONTENTS** for a book on earthquakes or engines or seasons or electricity.

... Keep **DATA SHEETS**: careful, written records and notes on any science experiment. Write the **QUESTION** (or problem) and the **HYPOTHESIS** before you begin, and a **SUMMARY** at the end.

... Write **WEATHER MYTHS** to explain weather conditions or any other phenomena that persons long ago might not have understood.

... Compile a *HANDBOOK of FIRST AID PROCEDURES* for a school, home, camping trip, ski lodge, or kids' clubhouse.

... Write **PERSONIFICATION TALES** about clouds, hailstones, tornados, tidal waves, trade winds, ocean currents, or blizzards.

... Write **INTERVIEW QUESTIONS** for interviewing a geologist, entomologist, microbiologist, chemist, hematologist, physicist, ichthyologist, pharmacist, meteorologist, or any other scientist.

... Make a **GLOSSARY** of plants, land forms, birds, arachnids, invertebrates, bones, reptiles, electrical terms, viruses, or any other topic you are studying. Draw 15 or more of each...then label and write the definition and/or distinguishing characteristics.

4 More Good Ideas....

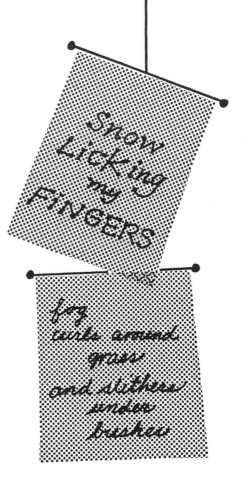

WEATHERGRAMS

A weathergram is a very short non-rhyming poem (10 words or less) that is not finished when you finish it. *It gets finished by the weather!* It is written **in permanent ink** (with very careful handwriting or calligraphy) on a 3 by 10 inch strip of biodegradable paper cut from a brown bag. Fold over the top, punch a hole, and thread it with a piece of twine. When the writing is done, hang the poem on a bush or branch in your yard, in the woods, or along a trail.

As it hangs outside, it is **finished** by the snow, wind, sun, and rain. With a few months of weathering, it becomes a true **weathergram**.

Write about something that has to do with nature, or the seasons, or the out-of-doors. Hang it in a place where passers-by can enjoy and ponder your brief thought. Do not sign your name, but make a small symbol or initial to mark it as yours.

PROMISES

Write lists of promises to keep, promises people **should** keep, promises you've broken...and so on...

Promises to Keep

To get to school on time
To be loyal to your friend
Not to tattle on people
To keep secrets
Not to talk to strangers
To go straight home from school
Not to do drugs
To change your underwear every day

Christina, Grade 2

Promises I've Broken

I promise...to practice the piano every day
I promise...to get to bed on time
I promise...to stay off the telephone tonight
I promise...to tell my parents where I'm going
I promise...to do my homework right away
I promise...to keep my room clean
I promise...not to torture my sister ever again
I promise...not to ski recklessly
I promise...I REALLY am too sick to go to school today

Isaac, Grade 8

I WONDER WHY....

There are so many things to wonder about. Write about them... in any form or genre...serious or silly...

I WONDER WHY SISTER IS MAD

I wonder why sis is so thoroughly mad
I don't understand it at all
Unless it's the frog on her closet floor
Or the nail in her favorite beach ball.

Perhaps it's the mustache that's drawn on her doll
Or the bubblegum stuck in her hair
Or the perfume of hers that got poured on the dog
Or the "whoopee" cushion placed on her chair.

Could it be the paint on her favorite stuffed cat?
Or the spaghetti sauce poured on her feet?
Or the ants that moved into her doll house last night?
Or the Vaseline on her toilet seat?

It can't be the raw egg that's cracked on her head
Or the goblins drawn on her wall
I wonder why sis is so thoroughly mad
I can't understand it at all!

two 5th graders with little sisters

ALPHABETICALLY SPEAKING

***B** was born with a bang!*
It's Bewitching
    Brainy
     and Beautiful!
***B** has a Billion in the Bank*
And Believes in the Bible.
It has seen a Bazooka
    in the Bayou
And a Bawdy Bartender
    on a Balcony.
***B** Buzzes, Bops, Bites and Blabbers.*
And it Beguiles,
    Bedazzles and Bewilders.
It's been a Bachelor and a Bigamist.
***B** is always on its Best Behavior,*
Except when it Blunders
    Into Bootlegging.
      Marguerite & Leon, Grade 5

Write a poem that shows off **one** letter of the alphabet. This is a wonderful way to learn new words. Use your dictionary to help you collect. Can you (or your class) do this with the whole alphabet?

If you're an astronaut,
you don't have to make your bed.

If you're the cook,
you can snoop in the refrigerator.

If you're driving the bulldozer,
no one bosses you around.

If you're the president,
you can be late.

Kara, Grade 4

236

12

INDEPENDENCE

"How can I get them to write on their own?"

In Celebration Of Independent Writing
How To Help Them Do It On Their Own
A Word Of Caution About Independent Writing Aids
A Permanent Writing Center For Your Classroom
Personal Journals For Kids And Teachers

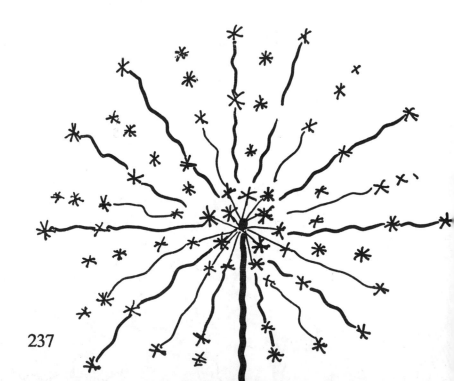

IN CELEBRATION OF INDEPENDENT WRITING

Jessica and Brie have been writing adventure stories all summer on Jessica's new computer.

Tom has slipped a limerick on his dad's desk every day for the last two weeks. (His dad creates one to send back to Tom now and then.)

Roberto and friends write and sell a little publication called, *What's New in the 'Hood?* to neighbors. They sell advertising space, too.

Students at Hawthorne School find little rhymes hanging on classroom doorknobs on Valentine's Day—left by a stealthy band of 1st graders.

8th graders at Keno Middle School write *Dear Blabby* letters and get advice from a team of anonymous "Advisors" (their peers).

Jose, a 6th grader at Franklin School, has started carrying on a correspondence in code with the principal.

Michele stashes a whole folder full of private poetry in the back of her desk.

Andrea and her brother Damian write a soccer newsletter with reviews of games, news, and jokes for their soccer friends.

Paul comes to school one morning and hands his 1st grade teacher an unsolicited poem written on a napkin (page 239). His mother testifies to his sole and spontaneous authorship of the piece.

Kids do it all the time. Without adult suggestion or supervision, they're writing profusely—original plays and puppet shows, letters to Santa Claus, letters to order stuff from magazines, sidewalk graffiti, invitations to secret club meetings, signs to hang in their lockers, original song lyrics, diary entries, private stories, charts of their accomplishments, love notes, hate notes, and secrets to pass.

Because I'm convinced that growth is stimulated and challenge is offered by teacher-initiated writing experiences, and because I rejoice for the good times kids have writing in the presence of a skilled

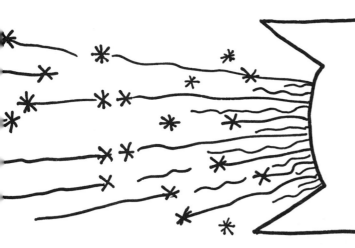

I understand
That the animals are not friendly
And the men of the world
Can be seen from miles away.

I see
The moon's lonely light
Will be there   Paul
Forever.   Age—almost 6

guide, this book has primarily outlined plans for launching and structuring group sessions. But such beliefs neither exclude the spontaneous nor assume that good writing emerges only from formal lessons. I applaud the self-initiated expressions of children and praise the teachers who encourage them.

For many years, I've observed and eavesdropped on skilled teachers who are able to keep alive the natural motivations to write. This is what I see those teachers doing...

... They provide time and avenues within the school day for independent writing.
... They encourage kids to start private journals, portfolios, diaries, collections, scrapbooks.
... They create settings in which students can share or tell about that personal writing.
... They do not assume that good writing happens only in school.
... They do their own independent writing (in ways that their students can notice):

    writing notes to kids
    writing notes to other teachers
    making signs and banners for their own desks
    writing personal reminders and sticking them on their desks
    posting a protest sign on occasion
    giving kids written (rather than oral) messages
    sharing some things they've written at home

HOW TO HELP THEM DO IT ON THEIR OWN

You'll get a head start on nurturing independence in writing when you heartily support and encourage the self-instigated writing kids are doing. Then what about continuing the process within the classroom?

BIAS #28
INDEPENDENCE CAN BE CULTIVATED

Freedom and time to write alone are the fertile soil. But teachers can offer a great deal more to nourish the growth of competent, autonomous writers. They can supply loads of affirmation. And they can teach kids processes and tools that will make independent writing exciting and fulfilling.

FIRST ... Be sure they write with a teacher-assisted group often enough to gain security in the writing process.

... Provide regular experiences with the writing process.

... Make aids and tools available that can be help writers with independent idea collecting, organizing, revising, and presenting. Keep these close at hand for easy use.

... Gather groups together often for mini-lessons on the skills they need for writing and rewriting on their own.

THEN ... They'll know what steps to follow: how to find ideas, stretch them, and change them into words.

... They'll know where to look for the help they need.

... They'll have their supplies packed for trekking off on independent writing adventures.

240

A WORD OF CAUTION ABOUT INDEPENDENT WRITING AIDS

I am an ardent crusader for individualized instruction, an avid user of learning centers, and a noisy advocate of independent writing.

BUT ... I have seen that *independent* or *individualized* aids to writing can be easily misused—or at least used in ways that diminish their value and don't help improve writing skills much.

I don't believe you **TEACH** a student to write on her own by sending her to a writing center (no matter how attractive or clever it may be). Nor do you increase writing abilities by handing kids a packet of Writing Starters to follow on their own (even if the starters are a collection of wonderful, inspiring ideas). Nor do you advance a student's writing skills by giving him a soup can full of inventive soup-related ideas and saying, *"Choose one."*

The soup can or the packet of motivators or writing center should not be, by themselves, the center of a plan for writing instruction. If kids are using such independent "aids," they need an introduction to them and they need to have a reason to use them. For instance...

> After a great tall tale party or whopper-writing session, the time may be ripe for starting a collection called, *YOU'LL NEVER BELIEVE THIS!* in your classroom Writing Center. You might ask that each student add one page to the collection.

OR

> A mouse trap with some attached writing ideas may seem irrelevant to students. But if the mouse trap appears the day you've shared your favorite *MICE* poems or the day after a mouse has been loose in the classroom, there will be a purpose and some relevance for writing about mice.

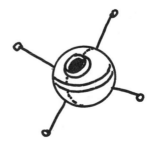

A PERMANENT WRITING CENTER FOR YOUR CLASSROOM

Every classroom can use a spot that centers on writing. You can call it a ... *Writer's Nook ... Scribe's Corner ... Editor's Desk...*

... Set it up behind a screen or bookcase ... in a large box ... under a canopy ... in a cozy corner ... or any spot with a comfortable place to sit and think and write.

... Furnish it with a writer's desk, preferably with drawers... shelves for storing writing supplies ... a bulletin board for ideas ... a large **Billboard** or **Gallery Wall** for showing off writing.

... Include an assortment of ideas ... activities ... suggestions ... writer's tools ... and motivators ready for use by writers.

... Keep it well-organized—with supplies stored in easy-to-reach, easy-to-store containers.

... Keep it changing and growing ... a place with a freely-flowing supply of fresh ideas, samples of good writing, sources of information, and assistance for using the writing processes and techniques.

242

Your Writing Center Might Include...

THINGS TO WRITE ON...

plain paper	old notebooks	floor tiles	file cards
newspaper	book covers	note pads	driftwood
lined paper	envelopes	old boxes	plastic bags
newsprint	cardboard tubes	slates	fabric scraps
graph paper	plastic tablecloths	rocks	window panes
cardboard	old window shades	chalkboards	wrapping paper
butcher paper	computer paper	sand	wood scraps
carbon paper	calculator tape	walls	shingles
paper bags	vinyl scraps	bricks	foam core
wallpaper	posterboard	bark	

THINGS TO WRITE WITH...

pencils	pens	cut-out words and letters
crayons	markers	rubber stamps
fingers	feathers	toothpicks
chalk	colored pencils	brushes and paints
computer	typewriter	charcoal
clay	visible inks	invisible inks

OTHER TOOLS...

thesaurus	word finder	dictionary
scissors	tape	rulers
clipboard	erasers	notebook rings
stapler	foil	tape recorder
glue	paper punch	string

Keep in this center the collections of words and compilations of ideas that the class has gathered in earlier writing lessons or word-play games. Students can use these as aids to writing. When they do this...

... motivation increases because they're writing with ideas and tools which they have created.

... independence is encouraged because they are finding help on their own.

... YOU are freed from the burden of being the sole source of ideas and assistance and inspiration.

... their writing is building on previous writing experiences—and that's what growth is all about!

243

More Stuff For Your Writing Center...

WRITER'S AIDS...

A Kid's Guide to the Writing Process
Editing/Revising Checklist
Questions To Ask for Response and Revision
Mechanics Checklist
Guide for Making a Book
Suggestions for Showing Off or Publicizing Writing
Rules and Helps for Spelling
Rules and Helps for Grammar and Mechanics
Addresses for Letter-Writing

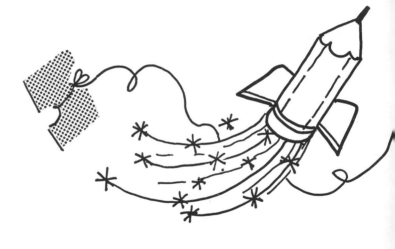

Word Lists: food words   color words   sound words
           people words   place words   smell words
           taste words   outdoor words   mysterious words   etc...

Forms or "Formulas" for different kinds of writing:
           limericks   cinquains   diamantes
           couplets   sonnets   business letters
           essays   haiku   friendly letters   etc...

Samples: advertisements   editorials   various poems
          announcements   invitations   dialogues
          headlines   telegrams   sports reports
          news articles   interviews   travel brochures
          posters   tall tales   applications
          menus   descriptions   speeches
          anecdotes   lyrics   directions   etc...

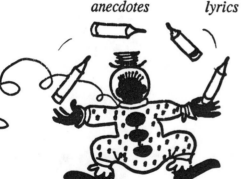

244

OTHER GOOD STUFF ...

*Classroom composite books to which students can add a page or a sample
or a poem or a word or a line ... Here are some sample titles...*

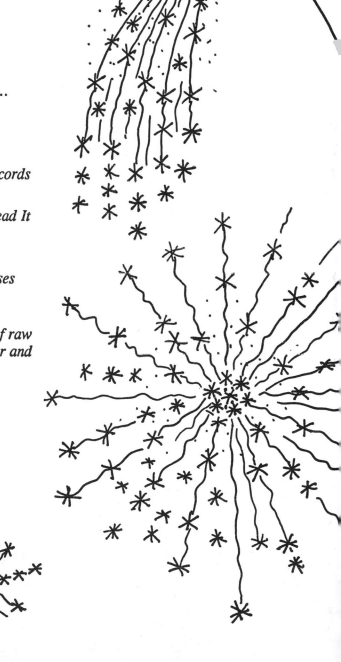

Lion Tales	*Close Encounters*
Things Kids Ought To Know	*HELP!*
Writing Good Enough To Eat	*Creature Features*
Back to the Future	*Places You Shouldn't Visit*
Imagine That!	*This Really Makes Me Mad...*
Rebus Stories	*Letters to the Principal*
Just Plain Good Advice	*Who's Who in Our School*
Our Undeniably Wise Sayings	*Yours Till...*
Our Own Book of Lists	*Our Own Book of World Records*
Slips of the Tongue	*You'll Never Believe This*
For Skiers Only	*Sports Like You've Never Read It*
Move Over, Shakespeare!	*Pet Shenanigans*
Who-Done-It?	*Our Dilly Dictionary*
Cures for Common Diseases	*Cures for Uncommon Diseases*

*Kids can also contribute to collections, not of finished writing, but of raw
material to stimulate other kids to write. They can come to the Center and
leave some of these for other writers...*

news headlines needing articles
news articles needing headlines
mysteries that need solving
cartoons needing captions
cliff-hangers without endings
jokes with missing punch lines
interview questions that need the answers
song titles without lyrics
song lyrics without titles
the missing half of a telephone conversation

245

PERSONAL JOURNALS FOR KIDS AND TEACHERS

> **BIAS #29**
> **PERSONAL WRITING MEETS HUMAN NEEDS**
> *One of the best reasons for writing on your own is that writing (even if—and especially when—it's not intended for an audience) serves well as a satisfying outlet for your feelings and ideas.*

It's a good way to try out your convictions, or get a clear look at a dilemma, or vent hostilities, or examine your fears, or think through a question, or articulate feelings. It's a good way to get to know yourself. And private writing lets you do all this without the risk of trying out thoughts on someone else!

Kids and teachers use journals in dozens of different ways. None of them are the **best** way for everyone. I do journal writing as a part of every classroom, under a process agreed-upon by teacher and students. Some thoughts to consider (these are **not** rules)...

- Get a notebook for each student—and for yourself.

- Dedicate 2, 5, or 10 minutes DAILY to private writing. Do it the same time every day for consistency OR choose different times, situations, and settings to catch a variety of moods and ideas.

- During journal-writing time, YOU WRITE TOO!

- Declare the journals off limits to everyone but the author.

- Let kids write in any form, on any topic.

- Each day, you might suggest an idea, (see next page), but don't force them. Reading plenty of literature supplies ideas, too.

- Encourage kids to carry journals around for collecting words, ideas, snatched phrases and sentences, overheard dialogues, etc.

- Share one of your journal entries now and then.

- Give opportunities for students to share theirs too, if they wish. Encourage, but don't push.

Often, you will find that something you intended only for yourself turns out to be so good in writing...you'll want to share it with others.

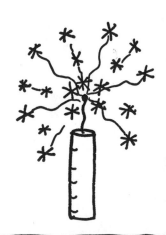

IDEAS for JOURNAL-WRITING...

joys
hurts
fears
memories
worries
compliments
sounds
noises
regrets
expectations
dilemmas
secrets

morning feelings
evening feelings
after-school feelings
dreams
wishes
disappointments
protests
close encounters
future plans
mistakes
opinions
pet peeves

sky watching
weather watching
people watching
animal watching
things worth saving
the news this morning
the way the world is
questions I can't answer
things I've missed

BIG ideas
little ideas
crazy ideas
unusual ideas
ordinary ideas
awful ideas
wonderful ideas

Guess what!!!
If only...
I wonder about...
I can't stand this...
I could never do without...
I wish I knew...
When I was little...
I wish I could say...
I'd like to change...
Places I'd like to visit...
It isn't fair...
I wonder why...
If I could do it over...

Things I know about
I can do this!...
Favorite words I just made up
Things I'd like to say to someone
People that I'm afraid of
Notes that someone will never read
The most important moment today
Someone who puzzles me
Someone who intrigues me
Someone who irritates me

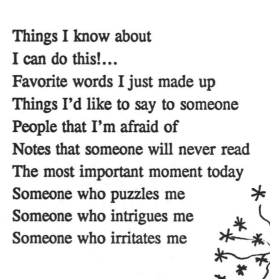

247

A Final Word

I live in the mountains of southern Oregon, and there's some pretty beautiful stuff to see around here. But, you know, a lot of time I'm inside working. And, unless I purposely stop and take time ... pulling myself away from the computer or the telephone ... I miss out on the great views in the wide outdoors.

You may not be catching the good views in your classroom, either. So ... STOP ... stand still with me a moment, and enjoy perusing the rewards of your work. Step back from the frenzy of working and sweating and climbing and watch just what it is that happens when you commit energy to nurturing expression.

FIRST ... behold how kids grow! They collect ideas with increasing enthusiasm, turn their impressions into words more easily, share their writing more freely, and express more openly. And isn't it a joy to glimpse those moments when they go beyond you—when their expectations surpass yours or they choose to gamble on their own ideas rather than rest safely on yours, or they venture into projects without prodding. You hear less of, "I can't think of anything," and more of, "Wait! I have another good idea."

And ... if you'll focus in closely, I think you'll notice that they're not just learning to write—they're learning to live! For the processes of organizing and directing thinking for writing sharpen skills needed for effectiveness in other areas of life. Those steps of collecting and sorting and organizing and censoring and evaluating are the same ones I use when I attempt to settle a dispute between two co-workers, or decide my position on a political issue, or prepare an agenda for a school board meeting. It's the very same process that's going on when I formulate (and rehearse) an apology (or an attack) to make to my husband after an argument, when I set arrangements for a trip, get a speech together for a workshop, gather my thoughts to make an important phone call, or plan a dinner for twenty people.

SECOND ... behold your own growth! A bonus of this whole writing-with-kids process is what happens to the teacher. I truly believe that you grow more than the kids! Your interest and your own effectiveness in written communication increase and you find yourself seeing possibilities in places you never thought to look. You change experiences into writing parties much more spontaneously and skillfully. Suddenly you're aware that your mouth knows what to ask and how to respond and what to suggest and when to be silent.

As with any venture into new territory—especially those territories of human expressions, values, and emotions—you take risks. You try new things of which you are uncertain, toy with motivators that will yield new inventions, bare some parts of your self as you grow and write with kids. Every time you start a new writing journey, you launch into uncharted waters, even if you've used the idea before—because a new group of kids and a new moment make it unlike any other experience. You can expect uncertainty from the students, too. There's apprehension any time someone creates a brand new thing. When students invent and share their thoughts and themselves, they risk disapproval, misunderstanding, disrespect—just as you risk a lack of response to your ideas, headshaking by the principal, disbelief of parents, or icy stares from the teacher nextdoor.

I encourage you to take the chances—and delight in them! For without them, you miss the rewards. Don't be afraid to keep inching out farther on the limb. If it starts to crack, you can retreat in search of a stronger one. But if you stay on the ground, you'll never see how the world looks from the top of that tree!

The risks will seem smaller ... the going will be more smooth ... if you will...

*... **Remember that it takes time.** Alice Bergstrom, Amy Glazer, and Erma Meisenheimer, three of my high school English teachers (back in the early 1960s), gave hours to the cultivation of my written expression. They sat with me dozens of times, revising drafts, praising, suggesting. I believe that their dedication and patience were key factors in the development of the literary appreciation, persistence, and self-discipline which I've called upon many times since high school. But here I am, many years later, still refining my writing skills! If, at the end of a school year, you're inclined to tear out your hair (or the kids' hair!) over still-rampant, run-on sentences or sloppy spelling or weak voice—DON'T! You cannot expect mastery from a second, sixth, or twelfth grader. Please don't berate yourself or the kids for the recurring weaknesses. **Learning to write is a lifelong process.** Sometimes we teachers forget that our year with a child is just one small piece of that lifetime process.*

*... **Trust the kids.** They can be guided to better writing. Relax and have faith in your ability to ask the right questions, propose relevant assignments, confront problems with wisdom.*

Ten years ago when Laura Keppner came to me with her paper and said, "Mrs. Frank, I can't think of anything else," I looked at her few dull sentences and—to be honest—I couldn't think of much either. So I put my arm around her shoulder and said, "Now Laura, if you go back to your desk and think real hard, I'm sure you'll come up with some more." Five years later when her brother, Kenny, raised his hand with the same complaint, my mouth erupted with so many suggestions that he finally covered his ears and said, "Okay, okay, that's enough!"

*And it was several years later that I became conscious of what had happened—I was not nearly so afraid of kids' questions or hesitations any more. Gradually my skill and confidence had grown, because I had talked to kids and eavesdropped on other teachers, scrounged ideas, tried some crazy things, suffered through some terrible flops, tried again, and listened to kids. And I have met scores of other teachers who have shared a similar growth. I don't believe we are unique. It happens to anyone who dedicates time and care to taking risks and writing with young people. **Writing WITH** young people ... not telling them what to do or worshipping any **system** ... but becoming a writer along with your students.*

*... **Give freely of yourself.** Every child working toward personal expression should enjoy the company of at least one grown-up who delights in hearing words bump into one another and who's willing to share his or her enthusiasm for life and discovery. I was fortunate enough to have a mother and a few other such adults in my childhood and adulthood. We can't count on that being the case for every child. **You may be that one adult for many of your students.** Don't let any one pass through your life or classroom without being touched by the power of written words. And as you give them this, you'll receive from them in return.*

I hope you will let yourself watch ... laugh ... cry ... and wonder at kids as they unfold their expressions to themselves, to you, to each other, and to life.

With my applause for your writing ventures, my hopes for your successes, and my empathies for your mistakes—(you can blame them on me)...

Marjorie Frank

and one more very good idea...

Several years ago, I was given an unexpected look at the Marjorie Frank of the past. My mom died suddenly, and as my father had been gone since I was a teenager, we four children set about the task of sorting through 65 years of our parents' belongings. As we sat on the basement floor of our mother's house, sniffling over diaries, laughing at old photographs, and bawling through our parents' love letters, I came upon a personal *time capsule*—a package Mother had saved and labeled as, "Marjorie's Writings." I read through poems, essays, and stories I hardly remembered writing, and got a surprise look at the fears, beliefs, and ideas of a grade school and high school kid who was myself. I was supplied with a precious hour of learning more about who I am and how I came to be the person I am today.

Personal Time Capsules are a great gift to offer yourself and your students. Fill a box or envelope with treasured stuff... some writing, important items, a photograph, and any other items or writings that tell about who the person is today. Secure it with sealing wax. Then label... **DO NOT OPEN UNTIL_____** and send it home to be stashed away for 5, 10, or 20 years.

TIME CAPSULE

Time Capsule

Today's date is_____

Presently, my life is_____

What I most like to do is_____

I value_____

Important people in my life are_____

_____

I get angry about_____

I wish I could change_____

My greatest joy is_____

Lately, I've hurt about_____

My best memory is_____

I worry about_____

Ten years from now, I hope to be_____

Before I die, I hope_____

Recently, I've learned_____

Something else special about me right now is_____

_____

251

INDEX

IDEA INDEX